Dedication

To, My parents, **Mr. Nitin Wagholikar** and **Mrs.Jyoti Wagholikar**

I would like to dedicate this book to my loving mother and father, who have been my constant source of support, encouragement, and inspiration throughout my journey of learning and proving myself to world.

My dear father **Mr. Nitin Wagholikar**, your guidance, wisdom, and technical expertise have been instrumental in fueling my curiosity and love for computers from an early age. You have nurtured my fascination with programming and instilled in me the importance of dedication and perseverance. This book is a testament to your profound influence on my journey.

My dear mother **Mrs.Jyoti Wagholikar,** your unwavering belief in my abilities and your endless encouragement have shaped me into the person I am today. Your love, patience, and sacrifices have been the driving force behind my pursuit of knowledge and my passion for Technology and writing. This book is a tribute to your unwavering faith in me.

After that I want to thank my Grandfather **Late Mr. Nanabhau Wagholikar** to build my skills of writing in childhood itself.

I am forever grateful for the countless hours you both spent listening to my quandaries, providing guidance when I stumbled, and celebrating my triumphs along the way. Your unwavering support has given me the strength to pursue my dreams, even in the face of challenges.

Thank you for believing in me when no one else did and for instilling in me the values of hard work, determination, and resilience. This book is dedicated to you, as a token of my love, appreciation, and gratitude.

With all my love and Gratitude,

Gauri Nitin Wagholikar

Dedication

To my dear parents, **Mr. Manish Patil** and **Mrs. Anita Patil**,
This book exists today because of your unwavering support and encouragement in every step of my journey.

You have been my pillars of strength, guiding me through life's challenges and inspiring me to reach for the stars. Your belief in my abilities has shaped me into the person I am today.

With heartfelt gratitude, I dedicate this book on C programming to both of you. it's possible because you both always there for me. You have instilled in me a passion for learning and a relentless pursuit of knowledge. Your unwavering faith in my abilities has given me the confidence to embark on this endeavor.

To aspiring learners, this book offers a comprehensive approach to understanding C programming. It provides clear explanations, practical examples, and exercises that encourage practice, enabling students to build a solid foundation in this vital programming language.

To all those who embark on this journey of learning, may this book serve as a guiding light, illuminating the path towards mastery of C programming. May it empower you to overcome obstacles, unlock your potential, and pave the way for a successful future.

Once again, I extend my deepest appreciation to my beloved parents, whose unwavering love and support have made this dream a reality. This book is a testament to your immeasurable impact on my life and the lives of those who will benefit from its teachings.
With love and gratitude,
Prachi Manish Patil

Foreword

It is with great pleasure that We write the foreword for this remarkable book on C programming. As we perused its pages, We was captivated by the author's dedication and their vision to provide students with a comprehensive resource to learn and master the fundamentals of this essential programming language.

In today's rapidly evolving technological landscape, proficiency in programming has become a vital skill for aspiring engineers and computer scientists. The ability to code in C opens doors to endless possibilities, serving as a stepping stone to innovation and problem-solving in various domains.

What sets this book apart is its emphasis on clarity and practicality. The author has skillfully crafted explanations that demystify complex concepts, making them accessible even to those approaching programming for the first time. The inclusion of numerous examples and exercises reinforces understanding, allowing readers to apply what they learn and solidify their knowledge.

Moreover, the book's unique feature of providing placement interview questions is truly commendable. By incorporating real-world scenarios and challenges, it prepares students to navigate the competitive landscape of the industry with confidence. This practical approach ensures that learners not only grasp the theoretical aspects but also develop the skills needed to excel in their professional pursuits.

To the readers who embark on this journey, We encourage you to embrace the knowledge presented within these pages. Take advantage of the exercises, challenge yourself, and persevere through any difficulties you may encounter. Remember, learning programming is a continuous process, and each step forward brings you closer to unlocking the vast potential within you.

We extend my heartfelt congratulations to the author for their exceptional work in creating this invaluable resource. May this book serve as a guiding light for students venturing into the realm of C programming, empowering them to become skilled programmers, problem solvers, and trailblazers in the digital age.

Miss Gauri Nitin Wagholikar
Software Engineer

Miss Prachi Manish Patil
Software Engineer, Entrepreneur

Intern Crowd

I am thrilled to introduce this book on C programming, powered by Intern Crowd. As an avid supporter of educational initiatives, I have had the pleasure of witnessing the transformative impact of collaborative efforts in the field of learning and development.

Intern Crowd, a platform dedicated to fostering talent and knowledge exchange, has played a crucial role in the creation of this book. Through their innovative approach of connecting aspiring authors with a community of skilled interns, they have cultivated an environment that nurtures creativity, collaboration, and expertise.

The result is evident within these pages. The content is meticulously crafted, offering a comprehensive yet accessible guide to understanding the fundamental concepts of C programming. It is a testament to the collective wisdom and dedication of the talented individuals who have contributed their time and expertise through the Intern Crowd platform.

What makes this book truly special is its practical approach. The authors have skillfully blended theoretical knowledge with real-world examples, providing readers with the tools to apply their learning in practical scenarios. This emphasis on hands-on experience fosters a deeper understanding of the subject matter and empowers learners to develop their problem-solving skills.

The collaboration between Intern Crowd and the author is further amplified by the inclusion of placement interview questions. This addition reflects a keen understanding of the industry's demands and the need for students to bridge the gap between academia and the professional world. By preparing readers for the challenges they may encounter during job interviews, this book equips them with a competitive edge.

I must commend the author for their dedication to producing this remarkable resource, and I extend my appreciation to Intern Crowd for their invaluable support in bringing this project to fruition. Together, they have created a synergy that showcases the potential of collaborative efforts in educational endeavors.

To the readers who embark on this learning journey, embrace the knowledge presented within these pages. Dive deep into the exercises, challenge yourself, and leverage the practical insights provided. By doing so, you will not only gain a solid foundation in C programming but also acquire the skills and confidence to navigate the ever-evolving landscape of technology.

I extend my warmest congratulations to the author and Intern Crowd for their remarkable achievement. May this book serve as a beacon of knowledge, empowering students to unlock their potential and embark on successful careers in the field of programming.

Prachi Manish Patil
Software Engineer, Entrepreneur

Preface

Welcome to the preface of this book on C programming. It is with great pleasure that I introduce you to this comprehensive resource designed to help students learn the essential concepts of C programming and prepare for their journey into the world of computer science.

Programming has become an integral part of our modern lives, driving innovation and shaping industries across the globe. Aspiring programmers need a solid foundation in programming languages to navigate the complexities of software development and contribute to technological advancements.

This book aims to bridge the gap between theoretical knowledge and practical application. It is designed to provide a clear and concise understanding of the fundamentals of C programming, enabling readers to grasp key concepts and develop problem-solving skills.

Each chapter is carefully crafted to present topics in a logical progression, starting from the basics and gradually building upon them. The content is supported by examples, exercises, and practice questions to reinforce understanding and encourage hands-on learning.

Additionally, this book goes beyond just teaching the concepts of C programming. It includes a section dedicated to helping students prepare for placement interviews. Recognizing the importance of real-world application, it equips readers with the knowledge and confidence to tackle industry-specific challenges and excel in job interviews.

Throughout this journey, the unwavering support of my parents, Mr. Manish Patil and Mrs. Anita Patil, has been a constant source of inspiration. Their belief in me and their encouragement have fueled my determination to create a resource that can benefit aspiring learners like yourself.

We Were also grateful for the collaboration with Intern Crowd, whose platform has provided a unique opportunity to collaborate with talented individuals and create a work that is enriched by diverse perspectives and expertise.

We would like to express my appreciation to all those who have supported me throughout this endeavor, including my family, friends, and mentors. Your unwavering belief in me has been invaluable.

We sincerely hope that this book serves as a valuable resource on your path to mastering C programming. May it empower you to unlock your potential and open doors to a rewarding career in the vast world of programming.

Happy learning!
Gauri Nitin Wagholikar, Prachi Manish Patil

Acknowledgements

We would like to express my sincere gratitude to Intern Crowd for their invaluable support in bringing this book to fruition. Their dedication and collaborative spirit have been instrumental in its creation. we were deeply grateful for the opportunity to work with such a talented and passionate team.
Thank you.
Gauri Nitin Wagholikar, Prachi Manish Patil

Prologue

In the realm of C programming, where logic meets syntax and creativity blends with problem-solving, lies the foundation of a fascinating journey. This prologue invites you to embark on an adventure through the intricacies of this powerful language.

C programming has been the cornerstone of software development for decades, serving as a gateway to numerous technological advancements. This prologue sets the stage, introducing you to the world of C, its significance, and the endless possibilities it holds.

Here, we delve into the fundamentals, exploring the building blocks of C programming and its role in shaping modern computing. From variables and data types to control structures and functions, each concept sets the stage for a deeper understanding of the language.

Through this prologue, you will catch a glimpse of the challenges and rewards that await you on this journey. You will begin to appreciate the art of problem-solving, the precision of coding, and the potential to create software that can transform the world.

Embrace the possibilities as you embark on this adventure, ready to uncover the secrets of C programming. With dedication and an open mind, you will navigate the complexities, overcome obstacles, and develop the skills to embark on a successful programming career.

Let the prologue be your guiding light, igniting the spark of curiosity and propelling you towards a profound understanding of C programming. May this introduction inspire you to embark on an exciting exploration of this remarkable language.

Welcome to the prologue of your C programming journey!

To My Partner-1

To my partner, **Miss Gauri Nitin Wagholikar,**

Congratulations on the completion of our dream! I am incredibly grateful for your immense support and assistance throughout the writing of this book. Your contributions have been invaluable, and I hold great respect for you.

Thank you for your unwavering dedication, hard work, and belief in our project. Together, we have achieved something remarkable. This book is a testament to our partnership and the fulfillment of our shared vision.

With heartfelt appreciation and admiration,
Prachi Manish Patil

To My Partner-2

To my partner, **Miss Prachi Manish Patil,**

I would like to extend my heartfelt gratitude to my incredible partner,and Best Friend Miss. Prachi Patil whose unwavering support and understanding have been instrumental in bringing this book to fruition. Your patience, encouragement, and belief in my abilities have been a constant source of motivation throughout this writing journey.

Thank you for lending me your ear during countless brainstorming sessions, offering valuable feedback, and providing a fresh perspective when I needed it most. Your unwavering belief in my vision and your unconditional love have been the pillars on which I built this book.

I am eternally grateful for your unwavering support, understanding, and for being my rock throughout this process. This book is as much yours as it is mine.

With all my love,
Gauri Nitin Wagholikar

CHAPTER ONE

Introduction to Programming

Introduction to Programming refers to the initial phase of learning about the fundamental principles and concepts of computer programming.

It is a foundational course designed to familiarize learners with the basic building blocks of programming languages and develop a problem-solving mindset.

In this introductory phase, learners gain an understanding of programming language syntax, program structure, and the overall process of writing and executing code.

They are introduced to key concepts such as variables, data types, control structures, and input/output operations.

This phase also emphasizes the importance of logical thinking, algorithmic problem-solving, and the use of programming languages as tools for creating software solutions.

Through hands-on exercises and projects, learners begin to develop their coding skills and learn how to approach and break down problems into smaller, manageable tasks.

The Introduction to Programming phase lays the groundwork for further exploration and specialization in specific programming languages and domains.

Overview of high level and low-level programming languages

High level programming languages:

A high-level programming language is a language designed to be easier for humans to read, write, and understand compared to low-level languages like assembly or machine code.

It provides a higher level of abstraction by using natural language constructs, meaningful variable names, and a syntax that resembles human languages.

High-level languages offer benefits such as improved readability, portability (ability to run on different platforms), increased productivity with built-in functions and libraries, and safety features like type checking and memory management.

They allow programmers to focus on the logic and algorithms of a program rather than low-level details. Examples of high-level languages include Python, Java, C++, JavaScript, Ruby, and C#.

These languages aim to make programming more accessible and efficient by providing powerful development environments and tools.

Low-level programming languages:

A low-level programming language is a language that is closer to the hardware and provides a direct representation of machine instructions.

It offers little or no abstraction from the underlying hardware architecture. Low-level languages are typically used for tasks that require fine-grained control over hardware resources, such as device drivers, operating systems, and embedded systems.

They are more difficult to read and write compared to high-level languages, as they require knowledge of the specific hardware and architecture being targeted.

Examples of low-level languages include assembly language and machine code. Programmers using low-level languages have direct access to memory, registers, and other hardware components, allowing for precise control and optimization.

Installation (Dev C++)

Introduction of (Dev c++):

- Dev-C++ is an Integrated Development Environment (IDE) for programming in C and C++.

- It provides a user-friendly editor, a compiler (MinGW GCC), a debugger, and project management capabilities.
- It offers a comprehensive development environment for writing, compiling, and debugging C and C++ programs, making it popular among both beginners and experienced programmers.

Installation (Dev C++):
The installation steps for Dev-C++:

- Visit the official Dev-C++ website: http://www.bloodshed.net/devcpp.html
- Download the latest version of Dev-C++ by clicking on the download link provided on the website.
- Once the download is complete, locate the downloaded setup file and double-click on it to start the installation process.
- Follow the on-screen instructions provided by the installer. You can choose the desired installation location and select additional components if needed.
- During the installation, you may be prompted to install additional software components required by Dev-C++. Follow the prompts and install any necessary components.
- After the installation is complete, you can launch Dev-C++ by finding its shortcut in the Start menu or desktop.
- Upon launching Dev-C++, you may be asked to configure the compiler settings. The default settings should work fine in most cases, but you can customize them according to your requirements.
- Once the configuration is done, you are ready to start coding in C and C++ using Dev-C++.

Introduction to the C programming language

- C is a general-purpose programming language developed in the early 1970s.
- It is a procedural language, which means it follows a step-by-step approach to solve problems.
- C provides a wide range of data types, operators, and control structures, allowing for efficient program execution and manipulation of data.
- It is known for its simplicity and efficiency, making it popular for system programming and embedded systems.
- C supports modular programming through functions and allows the reuse of code through libraries.
- It is a low-level language, providing direct access to memory and hardware resources.
- C is highly portable and can be compiled and executed on various platforms and architectures.
- It has a rich set of standard libraries that provide functions for tasks like input/output, string manipulation, and mathematical operations.
- C has influenced the development of many other programming languages, including C++, Java, and C#.

- It is widely used in operating systems, device drivers, embedded systems, game development, and scientific applications.

Why use C ?

Dennis Ritchie created the C programming language in the early 1970s, and that had a significant impact on the computing industry. Despite the emergence of numerous contemporary programming languages, C is still alive and well and is still an essential tool for software development across many different fields. We will examine the enduring and varied applications of the C language and highlight its importance in the current technological environment.

1. Systems Programming and Operating Systems:

Systems programming is one of the main areas where the C language shines. Its low-level nature makes it ideal for creating operating systems, device drivers, firmware, and embedded systems because it enables direct memory access and effective manipulation of hardware resources. C is widely used in well-known operating systems like UNIX, Linux, and Windows, underscoring its fundamental importance in this field.

2. Embedded Systems and IoT:
The direct hardware interaction capabilities of C and its effective resource management make it a top choice for developing embedded systems. C is the best language for applications requiring real-time responsiveness, low power consumption, and small code sizes because it enables developers to program with fine-grained control over system resources on a variety of platforms, including microcontrollers and IoT devices.

3. Game Development:
The gaming industry is still thriving, and C has made itself known there. C and C++ are used extensively in game engines like Unreal Engine and Unity. High-performance and graphically demanding games can be made thanks to C's performance-oriented design, control over memory management, and direct hardware access.

4. Networking and Protocol Development
The low-level networking capabilities of the C language make it the go-to language for creating network applications and protocols. C gives programmers the necessary control over network resources and effective data processing abilities, enabling them to build web servers and communication protocols like TCP(Tramission Control Protocol)/IP(Internet Protocol).

5. Scientific and Numeric Computing:

The language C is still widely used in scientific computing, despite the fact that it may not be the first to come to mind. In C, libraries like GSL (GNU Scientific Library) and FFTW (Fastest Fourier Transform in the West) are implemented, offering effective computational capabilities for math and numbers. The portability of C also enables researchers to run computationally demanding simulations and experiments on a variety of hardware platforms.

History of C

Before getting started with C programming, lets get familiarized with the language first. C is a general-purpose programming language used for wide range of applications from Operating systems like Windows and iOS to software that is used for creating 3D movies.

Since its inception, the C programming language, which is renowned for its ease of use effectiveness, and portability, has had a significant influence on the fields of computer science and software development. C, which Dennis Ritchie created at Bell Laboratories in the early 1970s, was instrumental in establishing the modern computing industry and is still a core programming language today.

C programming is highly efficient. Thats the main reason why its very popular despite being more than 40 years old. Standard C programs are portable. The source code written in one system works in another operating system without any change.

The history of C began in 1969, when Bell Laboratories employees Dennis Ritchie and Ken Thompson were working on the creation of the UNIX operating system. When Thompson realized the need for a higher-level language that could enable portability and ease of use across various computer architectures, he realized that an early version of UNIX had been written in assembly language.
History of C language is interesting to know. C programming language was developed in 1972 by Dennis Ritchie at bell laboratories of AT&T (American Telephone & Telegraph), located in U.S.A. Dennis Ritchie is known as the founder of C language.

It was developed to overcome the problems of previous languages such as B, BCPL etc. Initially, C language was developed to be used in UNIX operating system. It inherits many features of previous languages such as B and BCPL.

C is still relevant and widely used today. It is essential for low-level programming, high-performance computing, and applications that require direct hardware control because of its simplicity, performance, and variety of uses.

So, to conclude the C programming language has a long history of innovation, teamwork, and significant influence. C quickly gained popularity and turned into the preferred language for many software projects after it was created to meet the demands of the developing UNIX operating system.

C's legacy in computer science is solidified by its standardization, influence on succeeding languages, and pivotal role in enabling technologies. C's legacy endures as we continue to push the limits of technology, bearing witness to the foresight and inventiveness of its designers.

Features of C

1. Simple:
The C programming language is simple to use. It is suitable for both novice and seasoned programmers due to its simple syntax and understandable constructs. The languages primary goal is to make it simple and clear to express algorithms and solutions.

2. Machine Independent or Portable:
Being highly portable, C programs can be created once and run with little to no modification on a variety of platforms. Compilers for various operating systems and hardware architectures make C an excellent language for cross-platform development due to its portability.

3. Mid-Level Programming Language:
C is a mid-level programming language that combines low-level language efficiency and control with high-level language features. It is appropriate for a variety of applications because it allows direct manipulation of memory and hardware resources and offers constructs for modular and structured programming.

4. Structured Programming Language:
Programming in C is structured, with a focus on clean, modular code. It enables programmers to use functions and logical building blocks to transform complex issues into manageable structures. This method enhances the readability, maintainability, and reuse of the code. C programmers can write effective, well-structured programs that are simpler to comprehend and debug by using structured programming.

5. Rich Library:
There is a sizable selection of libraries for C that offer ready-to-use tools and functions for typical programming tasks. Input/output operations, string manipulation, calculations, networking, and other functionalities are just a few of the many topics covered by these libraries. Utilizing these libraries speeds up and simplifies development.

6. Memory Management:

C language provides manual memory management, allowing programmers to explicitly allocate and deallocate memory using functions like malloc() and free(). This feature gives developers fine-grained control over memory usage, enabling efficient utilization of system resources. However, it also requires careful management to prevent memory leaks or segmentation faults.

7. Fast Speed:
The compiled nature of the C language, which is well known for its quick speed, makes it ideal for performance-critical applications.

8. Pointers:
One of the core components of the C language are pointers. They allow for effective memory management, direct memory manipulation, and parameter passing by reference. For tasks like dynamic memory allocation and creating intricate data structures, pointers are crucial.

9. Recursion:
A function can call itself by using C's powerful recursion feature. By dividing complex problems into smaller, more manageable subproblems, it makes it possible to solve them. Recursive functions have a base case that ends recursion and calls that solve smaller instances of the same problem in a recursive manner. For problems that can be solved elegantly and effectively through recursion, this method is used.

10. Extensible:
A function can call itself thanks to the C language's powerful recursion feature. By dividing complex issues into smaller, easier to handle problems, it makes it possible to solve complex issues. Recursive functions have a base case that stops recursion as well as recursive calls that address smaller instances of the same issue. For tasks that can be expressed recursively, this technique offers an elegant and effective solution.

Exercise - 1

1. Explain the difference between high-level and low-level programming languages. Give examples of each.

2. How do you install Dev C++ on your computer? Provide step-by-step instructions.

3. What are the basic components of a C program? Explain each component briefly.

4. Why is C considered a popular programming language? List some advantages of using C.

5. Provide a brief overview of the history of the C programming language. Who created it and when?

6. What are the key features of the C programming language that make it widely used in various domains?

7. Describe the concept of variables in C. How are variables declared and used in C programs?

8. Explain the significance of control structures in C programming. Give examples of different control structures.

9. What are functions in C? How are they defined and used? Provide an example of a function in C.

10. Discuss the importance of data types in C. Provide examples of different data types and their uses.

CHAPTER TWO

Basics of C programming

Before Starting the Actual Coding in C Programming Language let's understood what exact it is- Communicating with a computer requires speaking a language that the computer understands, so English is immediately dismissed as a language for communicating with a computer. However, learning English is very similar to learning C. The classic way of learning English is to first learn the alphabet used in that language, then learn to combine these alphabets to form words, then combine the words to form sentences. And then learn to make sentences.

Learning C is similarly easy. Instead of immediately learning how to write programs, you'll first learn what special letters, numbers, and symbols are used in C, then how to construct constants, variables, and keywords. And finally, we need to know how these fit together to form a program. Order. Groups of instructions are later combined to form programs.
   We can get more clearification by reviewing below diagram:

Group Of Instructions For C Program

Structure Of C

Before we study the basic building blocks of the C programming language,

let us look at a bare minimum C program structure so that we can take it

as a reference.

A C program basically consists of the following parts -

1. Preprocessor Commands

2. Functions

3. Variables

4. Statements & Expressions

5. Comments

Let us look at a **simple code** that would print the words "Hello World"

```
#include<stdio.h>

int main(){

/*my first program in C */

printf("Hello World!");

return 0;

}
```

Let us take a look at the various parts of the above program -

- The first line of the program #include <stdio.h> is a preprocessor command, which tells a C compiler to include stdio.h file before going to actual compilation. The printf() function is defined in stdio.h The next line int main() is the main function where the program execution
- begins. . The next line /.../ will be ignored by the compiler and it has been put to add additional comments in the program. So such lines are called
- comments in the program. The next line printf(...) is another function available in C which causes the message "Hello, World!" to be displayed on the screen. .
- The next line return o; terminates the main() function and returns the value 0.

Flow of C Program

The C Program Follows many steps in execution. To understand the flow of C program well, Let us see a simple Program

File: Simple.c

```
#include<stdio.h>

void main(){

Printf("Hello InternCrowd!");

}
```

Let's try to understand the Flow of above program by the figure given below:

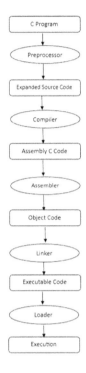

Execution Of C Language Code

1) C program (source code) is sent to preprocessor first. The preprocessor is responsible to convert preprocessor directives into their respective values. The preprocessor generates an expanded source code.

2) Expanded source code is sent to compiler which compiles the code and converts it into assembly code.

3) The assembly code is sent to assembler which assembles the code and converts it into object code. Now a simple.obj file is generated.

4) The object code is sent to linker which links it to the library such as header files. Then it is converted into executable code. A simple.exe file is generated.

5) The executable code is sent to loader which loads it into memory and then it is executed. After execution, output is sent to console.

Prinf, Scanf in C

The **printf() and scanf()** functions are used for input and output in C language. Both functions are inbuilt library functions, defined in stdio.h (header file)

Printf() and Scanf() Function :

C does not contain any instruction to display output on the screen. All output to screen is achieved using readymade library functions. One such function is printf().

The printf() function is used for output. It prints the given statement to the console. The syntax of printf() function is given below:

printf("format string", argument_list);

The format string can be %d (integer), %c (character), %s (string), % f(float), %ld(double float) etc.

Scanf() Function:

In the C programming language, scanf is a function that stands for **Scan Formatted String**. It is used to read data from stdin (the standard input stream, usually the keyboard) and write the result to the given arguments. Accepts character, string, and numeric data from the user using standard input.

It reads data from the console. The syntax of scanf() function is given below:

scanf("format string", arugment_list);

Let us understand the function with the help of the program

Program to print sum of 2 numbers

Let's see a simple example of input and output in C language that prints addition of 2 numbers.

include<stdio.h>

include<conio.h>

int x=0, y=0, result=0;

printf("Please enter first number:");

scanf("%d", &x) ;

```c
printf("Please enter second number:");

scant("%d", &y);

result=x+y;

printf("Sum of Two numbers is :%d", result);

}
```

Output :

Please enter first number:3

Please enter second number:10

Sum of Two numbers is: 13

Let us understand by the **explanation of the code:**

1. Including Header Files:

#include <stdio.h>

The `stdio.h` header file is included, which provides standard input/output functions like `printf()` and `scanf()`.

2. Variable Declarations:

int x = 0, y = 0, result = 0;

Three integer variables are declared: `x`, `y`, and `result`. They are initialized to 0.

3. Prompting for the First Number:

```c
printf("Please enter the first number: ");
scanf("%d", &x);
```

The program displays the message "Please enter the first number: " using `printf()`. The user is expected to enter a number, which is then stored in the variable `x` using `scanf()`.

4. Prompting for the Second Number:

```c
printf("Please enter the second number: ");
scanf("%d", &y);
```

Similarly, the program prompts the user to enter the second number and stores it in the variable `y`.

5. Calculating the Sum:

result = x + y;

The program adds the values of `x` and `y` together and stores the result in the variable `result`.

6. Displaying the Result:

printf("Sum of the two numbers is: %d\n", result);

The program prints the message "Sum of the two numbers is: " followed by the value of `result` using `printf()`.

7. Program Termination:

return 0;

The `return 0` statement indicates that the program has executed successfully and terminates the program.

This code prompts the user to enter two numbers, calculates their sum, and then displays the result on the screen.

Basic Syntax of C

We have seen the basic structure of a C program, so it will be easy to understand other basic building blocks of the C programming language.

Tokens in C

AC program consists of various tokens and a token is either a keyword, an identifier, a constant, a string literal, or a symbol. For example, the following C statement consists of five tokens -

printf("Hello, world!"\n);

The individual tokens are:

1. printf

2.(

3."Hello World!"

4.)

5. ;

Semicolons

In a C program, the semicolon is a statement terminator. That is, each individual statement must be ended with a semicolon. It indicates the end of one logical entity.

Given below are two different statements -

printf("Hello, world!"\n);

return 0;

Comments

Comments are like helping text in your C program and they are ignored by the compiler. They start with /* and terminate with the characters */

as shown below -

/*My First Program In C*/

You cannot have comments within comments and they do not occur within a string or character literals.

Identifiers

AC identifier is a name used to identify a variable, function, or any other user-defined item. An identifier starts with a letter A to Z, a to z, or an underscore followed by zero or more letters, underscores, and digits (0 to 9).

C does not allow punctuation characters such as @, S, and % within identifiers. C is a case-sensitive programming language. Thus, Manpower and manpower are two different identifiers in C. Here are some examples of acceptable identifiers -

mohd	zara	abc	Move_name	a_345
myname	_temp	j	a23b7	retvai

List of Identifer

Keywords

The following list shows the reserved words in C. These reserved words may not be used as constants or variables or any other identifier names.

auto	else	long	Switch
break	enum	register	typedef
case	extern	return	Union
char	float	short	Unsigned
const	for	signed	Void
continue	goto	sizeof	Volatile
default	if	static	White
do	int	struct	double

List of Keywords

Comments

Comments in C are used to add explanatory or descriptive text within the source code. They are ignored by the compiler and do not have any impact on the execution of the program. Comments are useful for documenting code, providing explanations, or temporarily disabling code during development. There are two types of comments in C: single-line comments and multi-line comments.

1. Single-line comments: Single-line comments begin with // and continue until the end of the line. Anything written after // is considered a comment and is ignored by the compiler.

// This is a single-line comment
int x = 5; // This comment describes the purpose of the variable

2. Multi-line comments: Multi-line comments, also known as block comments, begin with /* and end with */. They can span multiple lines and are often used for longer comments or to comment out a block of code.

```
/*
* This is a multi-line comment.
* It can span multiple lines.
* These comments are commonly used to provide
* detailed explanations or disable sections of code.
*/
int y = 10; /* This code is commented out */
```

Comments are not only helpful for other developers who read and maintain the code but also for your own future reference. They improve code readability and help in understanding the logic and purpose of different parts of the program.

Here are some best practices for using comments effectively:

- Use comments to explain complex or non-obvious code sections.
- Provide high-level descriptions of functions, algorithms, or logic.
- Comment important decisions, assumptions, or limitations.
- Avoid excessive or redundant comments that simply restate the code.
- Update comments when making changes to the code to keep them accurate.
- Remove unnecessary comments before finalizing the code for production.

Exercise - 2

1. What is the purpose of using structures in C? Provide an example of a structure declaration and explain its components.
2. Write a program to print "Hello World!".
3. Write program to add two numbers using scanf and printf.
4. Write a C program that declares a structure called "" with the following members: name (string), age (integer), and height (float). Initialize the structure with data and print the values of its members using printf.
5. Discuss the importance of comments in C programs. Provide examples of single-line and multi-line comments in C.
6. Write a C program to print even number in 1 to 100.
7. Write a Program in C to print Your name.

CHAPTER THREE

Data Types

Introduction of data types in c:

Data types are used to define the type and size of data that can be stored in variables. Data types determine the operations that can be performed on the variables and the amount of memory required to store them.

Why we need data types in C:

Computers store data in binary numbers and allocate memory to each piece of data. Suppose you want to create a program to store your name, age, and phone number. Without specifying the data types, the computer would treat them equally, assigning the same memory to all of them.

However, the age typically consists of 2 to 3 digits, while a phone number has at least 10 digits. If the computer assigned the same memory to both, it would result in significant memory wastage.

To address this issue, we use data types to specify the type of data each variable represents. This prevents confusion and optimizes memory usage.

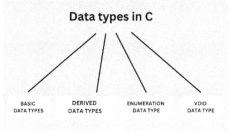

Data types in C Programming

Here are some of the commonly used data types in C:

1). Basic data types: The basic data types are also known as the **primitive data types** in C programming.

Primitive data types are the fundamental data types provided by the language itself. They are called "primitive".

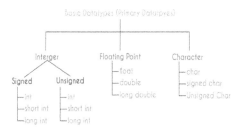

Basic Datatypes

a). Integer Data Types:

- **int**: This data type is used to store whole numbers. It typically occupies 4 bytes of memory.

Example: int count = 10;

Syntax:

The syntax of declaring a variable with the 'int' data type in C is as follows:

int variableName;

Here, 'int' is the keyword that specifies the data type as integer, and 'variableName' is the name you choose for the variable.

You can also initialize the 'int' variable at the time of declaration:

int variableName = initialValue;

In the above syntax, 'initialValue' represents the initial value assigned to the 'int' variable.

Here are a few examples of declaring and initializing 'int' variables:

int age;

int count = 0;

int temperature = 25;

In the first example, we declare an int variable named age without initializing it. In the second example, we declare and initialize an int variable named count with an initial value of 0. In the third example, we declare and initialize an int variable named temperature with an initial value of 25.

Example of int:

```
#include <stdio.h>
int main() {
int age = 15;
int count = 9;
int sum = age + count;
    printf("Age: %d\n", age);
printf("Count: %d\n", count);
printf("Sum: %d\n", sum);
    return 0;
}
```

Explanation of Example:-

In this example, we have declared and initialized three 'int' variables: 'age', 'count', and 'sum'.

The variable 'age' is assigned a value of 15, indicating a person's age. The variable 'count' is initialized with a value of 9. We then calculate the sum of 'age' and 'count' and store the result in the 'sum' variable.

Finally, we use 'printf()' to display the values of 'age', 'count', and 'sum' on the console. The '%d' format specifier is used to print integer values.

When you run this program, the **output** will be:

Age: 15

Count: 9

Sum: 24

- **char:** This data type is used to store individual characters. It occupies 1 byte of memory.

Example: char grade = 'A';

Syntax:

The syntax of declaring a variable with the 'char' data type in C is as follows:

char variableName;

Here, 'char' is the keyword that specifies the data type as character, and 'variableName' is the name you choose for the variable.

You can also initialize the 'char' variable at the time of declaration:

char variableName = initialValue;

In the above syntax, 'initialValue' represents the initial value assigned to the 'char' variable.

Here are a few examples of declaring and initializing 'char' variables:

char grade; char letter = 'A'; char symbol = '$';

In the first example, we declare a 'char' variable named 'grade' without initializing it. In the second example, we declare and initialize a 'char' variable named 'letter' with the initial value of 'A'. In the third example, we declare and initialize a char variable named symbol with the initial value of '$'.

Note That: The 'char' data type is used to store individual characters and occupies 1 byte of memory in most implementations of C. Characters are enclosed within single quotes '',
while strings are enclosed within double quotes '"'.

Example of char:

```
#include <stdio.h>
int main() {
char letter = 'A';
char symbol = '$';
char newline = '\n';
    printf("Letter: %c\n", letter);
printf("Symbol: %c\n", symbol);
printf("Newline Character: %c", newline);
    return 0;
}
```

Explanation of Example:-

In this example, we declare and initialize three variables of type 'char': 'letter', 'symbol', and 'newline'.

The 'letter' variable is assigned the character 'A', which represents an uppercase letter. The 'symbol' variable is initialized with the character '$', which represents a special symbol. The 'newline' variable is assigned the escape sequence '\n', which represents a newline character.

We then use 'printf()' to display the values of these 'char' variables. The '%c' format specifier is used to print 'char' values.

When the program is executed, it will **output:**

Letter: A

Symbol: $

Newline Character:

- **short:** This data type is used to store small integers. It usually occupies 2 bytes of memory.

Example: short temperature = -5;

Syntax:

The syntax of declaring a variable with the 'short' data type in C is as follows:

short variableName;

Here, 'short' is the keyword that specifies the data type as a short integer, and 'variableName' is the name you choose for the variable.

You can also initialize the 'short' variable at the time of declaration:

short variableName = initialValue;

In the above syntax, 'initialValue' represents the initial value assigned to the 'short' variable.

Here are a few examples of declaring and initializing 'short' variables:

short temperature;

short count = 100;

short year = -2022;

In the first example, we declare a 'short' variable named 'temperature' without initializing it. In the second example, we declare and initialize a 'short' variable named 'count' with an initial value of 100. In the third example, we declare and initialize a 'short' variable named 'year' with an initial value of -2022.

Note That: The 'short' data type is used to store small integers and typically occupies 2 bytes of memory in most implementations of C. The exact range of values that can be stored in a 'short' variable depends on the platform, but it is usually from -32,768 to 32,767.

Example of short:

```
#include <stdio.h>
int main() {
short temperature = -5;
short count = 100;
short sum = temperature + count;
    printf("Temperature: %hd\n", temperature);
printf("Count: %hd\n", count);
printf("Sum: %hd\n", sum);
    return 0;
}
```

In this example, we declare and initialize three variables of type 'short': 'temperature', 'count', and 'sum'.

The 'temperature' variable is assigned a value of -5, which represents a temperature in degrees. The 'count' variable is initialized with a value of 100, indicating a count of something.

We then perform an addition operation using the '+' operator and assign the result to the 'sum' variable.

Finally, we print the values of 'temperature', 'count', and 'sum' using 'printf()'. The '%hd' format specifier is used to print 'short' values.

When the program is executed, it will **output**:

Temperature: -5

Count: 100

Sum: 95

- **long**: This data type is used to store large integers. It generally occupies 4 bytes or more, depending on the platform.

Example: long population = 1000000L;

Syntax:

The syntax of declaring a variable with the 'long' data type in C is as follows:

long variableName;

Here, 'long' is the keyword that specifies the data type as a long integer, and 'variableName' is the name you choose for the variable.

You can also initialize the 'long' variable at the time of declaration:

long variableName = initialValue;

In the above syntax, 'initialValue' represents the initial value assigned to the 'long' variable.

Here are a few examples of declaring and initializing 'long' variables:

long population;

long distance = 10000L;

long largeNumber = 1234567890L;

In the first example, we declare a 'long' variable named 'population' without initializing it. In the second example, we declare and initialize a 'long' variable named 'distance' with an initial value of 10000, suffixed with 'L' to indicate a 'long' literal. In the third example, we declare and initialize a 'long' variable named 'largeNumber' with a large initial value.

Note That:- The 'long' data type is used to store large integers and occupies 4 bytes or more, depending on the platform. The exact range of values that can be stored in a 'long' variable depends on the platform, but it is typically larger than the range of 'int' or 'short'.

Note That: For 'long' variables, the suffix 'L' or 'l' can be added to literal values to indicate that they should be treated as 'long' integers.

Example of Long:

```
#include <stdio.h>
int main() {
long num1 = 1234567890;
long num2 = -9876543210;

printf("num1: %ld\n", num1);
printf("num2: %ld\n", num2);

return 0;
}
```

In this example, we declare two variables num1 and num2 of type long. The long data type is used to represent signed integers with a larger range compared to int. It typically has a minimum range of -2,147,483,648 to 2,147,483,647, but its actual size may vary depending on the system.

We assign values to num1 and num2, and then use the %ld format specifier in the printf function to print their values. The %ld format specifier is used specifically for long data types.

When you run this code, the output will be:

num1: 1234567890

num2: -9876543210

2). Floating-Point Types:

float: This data type is used to store single-precision floating-point numbers. It occupies 4 bytes of memory.

Example: float pi = 3.14f;

Syntax:- The syntax of declaring a variable with the 'float' data type in C is as follows:

float variableName;

Here, 'float' is the keyword that specifies the data type as a single-precision floating-point number, and 'variableName' is the name you choose for the variable.

You can also initialize the 'float' variable at the time of declaration:

float variableName = initialValue;

In the above syntax, 'initialValue' represents the initial value assigned to the 'float' variable.

Here are a few examples of declaring and initializing 'float' variables:

float pi;

float temperature = 25.5f;

float salary = 1000.75f;

In the first example, we declare a 'float' variable named 'pi' without initializing it. In the second example, we declare and initialize a 'float' variable named 'temperature' with an initial value of 25.5, suffixed with 'f' to indicate a 'float' literal. In the third example, we declare and initialize a float variable named salary with an initial value of 1000.75.

Note That: The 'float' data type is used to store single-precision floating-point numbers, which typically occupy 4 bytes of memory. Floating-point literals are written with a decimal point, even if the fractional part is zero, to indicate that they are floating-point values.

Note That: For 'float' variables, the suffix 'f' or 'F' can be added to literal values to indicate that they should be treated as 'float' values.

Example of float:

```
#include <stdio.h>
int main() {
float pi = 3.14159f;
float radius = 2.5f;
float area = pi * radius * radius;
    printf("Pi: %.5f\n", pi);
printf("Radius: %.2f\n", radius);
printf("Area: %.2f\n", area);
    return 0;
}
```

In this example, we declare and initialize three variables of type 'float': 'pi', 'radius', and 'area'.

The 'pi' variable is assigned the value of '3.14159f', which represents the mathematical constant Pi. The 'radius' variable is initialized with a value of '2.5f', representing the radius of a circle.

We then calculate the area of the circle using the formula 'area = pi * radius * radius' and assign the result to the 'area' variable.

Finally, we print the values of 'pi', 'radius', and 'area' using 'printf()'. The '%.5f' format specifier is used to print 'float' values with 5 decimal places, and the '%.2f' format specifier is used to print 'float' values with 2 decimal places.

When the program is executed, it will **output**:

Pi: 3.14159

Radius: 2.50

Area: 19.63

double: This data type is used to store double-precision floating-point numbers. It occupies 8 bytes of memory.

Example: double distance = 10.5;

Example of double:
```
#include <stdio.h>
int main() {
double num1 = 3.14159;
double num2 = -2.71828;

printf("num1: %lf\n", num1);
printf("num2: %lf\n", num2);

return 0;
}
```
Explanation of code:

In this example, we declare two variables num1 and num2 of type double. The double data type is used to represent floating-point numbers with double precision. It typically occupies 8 bytes of memory.

We assign values to num1 and num2, and then use the %lf format specifier in the printf function to print their values. The %lf format specifier is used specifically for double data types.

When you run this code, the output will be:

num1: 3.141590

num2: -2.718280

long double: This data type is used to store extended precision floating-point numbers. Its size can vary across platforms.

Example: long double preciseNum = 12345.67890L;

Program:
```
#include <stdio.h>
int main() {
long double pi = 3.14159265358979323846264338327950288L;
long double radius;
long double area;
printf("Enter the radius of a circle: ");
scanf("%Lf", &radius);
area = pi * radius * radius;
printf("The area of the circle is: %Lf\n", area);
return 0;
}
```
Explanation:

In this program, we declare a long double variable named pi to store the value of pi with extended precision. We then prompt the user to enter the radius of a circle and store the input in the long double variable radius.

The area of the circle is calculated using the formula area = pi * radius * radius, and the result is stored in the long double variable area. Finally, we print the calculated area using the %Lf format specifier, which is used specifically for long double values.

Note that: The %Lf format specifier is used for both input and output when dealing with long double values.

Void Type:

void: This data type is used to indicate the absence of a type. It is commonly used as a return type for functions that do not return a value.

Example:

```
void printMessage()
{
printf("Hello, World!\n");
}
```

Program:

```
#include <stdio.h>
// Function declaration with void return type and no parameters
void greet() {
printf("Hello, world!\n");
}
// Function declaration with void return type and an int parameter
void printNumber(int num) {
printf("The number is: %d\n", num);
}
int main() {
greet(); // Call greet() function
printNumber(42); // Call printNumber() function with an argument
return 0;
}
```

Explanation:

In this program, we have two functions: greet() and printNumber(). Both functions have a return type of void, indicating that they do not return any value.

The greet() function simply prints "Hello, world!" to the console.

The printNumber() function takes an integer parameter num and prints its value to the console.

In the main() function, we call greet() to display the greeting message and printNumber(42) to print the number 42.

Note that: while void is commonly used for functions that do not return a value, it can also be used as a data type for function parameters or pointers to functions.

Boolean Type:

_Bool: This data type is used to store boolean values, which are either 0 (false) or non-zero (true). It occupies 1 byte of memory.

Example: _Bool isTrue = 1;

It's worth noting that the sizes of these data types can vary depending on the platform and compiler being used. The sizeof operator can be used to determine the size of a specific data type on a given system.

Programs on Data Types

1. Program that finds the size of different data types in C:

```c
#include <stdio.h>

int main()

{
printf("Size of char: %lu byte(s)\n", sizeof(char));
printf("Size of int: %lu byte(s)\n", sizeof(int));
printf("Size of float: %lu byte(s)\n", sizeof(float));
printf("Size of double: %lu byte(s)\n", sizeof(double));
printf("Size of long: %lu byte(s)\n", sizeof(long));
printf("Size of long long: %lu byte(s)\n", sizeof(long long));
printf("Size of short: %lu byte(s)\n", sizeof(short));

return 0;
}
```

Output:

```
Size of char: 1 byte(s)
Size of int: 4 byte(s)
Size of float: 4 byte(s)
Size of double: 8 byte(s)
Size of long: 8 byte(s)
Size of long long: 8 byte(s)
Size of short: 2 byte(s)
```

Explanation:

In this program, the sizeof operator is used to find the size of each data type. The %lu format specifier is used to print the size as an unsigned long integer. The sizeof operator returns the size of a data type in bytes. The program prints the size of char, int, float, double, long, long long, and short data types.

2. Program to show type conversion in C.

```c
#include <stdio.h>

int main() {
int num1 = 10;
float num2 = 3.5;
int result;
```

```
result = num1 + (int)num2;

printf("Result: %d\n", result);

return 0;
}
```

Explanation:

This program showcases type conversion in C. The variable num1 is an integer, while num2 is a float. The (int) type cast is used to convert num2 to an integer before performing the addition. The result is then stored in the result variable and printed using the %d format specifier.

3. Program to Swap Two Numbers

```
#include <stdio.h>

int main() {
int num1 = 5;
int num2 = 10;
int temp;

printf("Before swapping: num1 = %d, num2 = %d\n", num1, num2);

temp = num1;
num1 = num2;
num2 = temp;

printf("After swapping: num1 = %d, num2 = %d\n", num1, num2);

return 0;
}
```

Output:

Before swapping: num1 = 5, num2 = 10
After swapping: num1 = 10, num2 = 5
Explanation: This program demonstrates swapping two numbers using a temporary variable. Two integers, num1 and num2, are initialized with values 5 and 10, respectively. The values are swapped using the temporary variable temp, and the results are printed before and after the swap.

Exercise- 3

Practice programming questions on data types:

1. Write a program to find the size of various data types (int, float, double, char) in C.

2. Write a program that accepts an integer input and displays its binary representation.

3. Write a program to swap two integers without using a temporary variable.

4. Write a program to convert a decimal number to its binary equivalent using bitwise operators.

5. Write a program to find the maximum and minimum values of the data types int, float, and double.

6. Write a program to check if a given number is a power of 2 using bitwise operators.

7. Write a program to reverse a given integer number and check if it is a palindrome.

8. Write a program to convert a given character to its corresponding ASCII value.

9. Write a program to find the factorial of a given number using recursion.

10. Write a program to calculate the sum of digits in a given integer number.

CHAPTER FOUR

Variable In C

A variable is a name of memory location. It is used to store data. Its value can be changed and it can be reused many times. It is a way to represent memory location through symbol so that it can be easily identified.

Let's see the syntax to declare a variable:

type variable_list;

The example of declaring variable is given below:

int a;

float b;

char c;

Here, a, b, c are variables and int, float, char are data types. We can also provide values while declaring the variables as given below:

int a=10,b=20 //declaring 2 variables for interger type

float f=20.8;

char c='A';

Rules for defining variables:

- A variable can how alphabets, digits and underscore.
- A variable name can start with alphabet and underscore only it can't start with digit
- No whitespace is allowed within variable name
- A variable name must not be any reserved word or keyword eg. int, float ,etc.

Valid variable names:

int a ;

int _ab;

inta50;

Inalid variable names:

int 2;

int a b;

int long;

Types of Variables in C

There are many types of variables in c

1. local variable
2. global variable
3. static variable
4. automatic variable
5. external variable

let's undestand one by one :

1. Local Variable

A variable that is declared inside the function or block is called local variable. It must be declared at the start of the block.

Example:

void function(){

int x=10; //local variable

}

You must have to initialize the local variable before it is used.

2. Global Variable

A variable that is declared outside the function or block is called global variable. Any function can change the value of the global variable. It is available to all the functions. It must be declared at the start of the block.

Example:
```
int value=20; //global variable
void function(){
int x=10 //local variable
}
```

3. Static Variable:

A variable that is declared with static keyword is called static variable. It retains its value between multiple function calls.

Example:
```
void function1(){
int x=10; //local variable
static int y=90; //static variable
x= x+1;
y=y+1;
printf("%d. %d" ,x,y);
}
```

If you call this function many times, local variable will print the same value for each function call e.g. 11,11,11 and so on. But static variable will print the incremented value in each function call e.g. 11, 12, 13 and so on.

4. Automatic Variable

All variables in C that is declared inside the block, are automatic variables by default. By we can explicitly declare automatic variable using auto keyword.

Example:
```
void main(){
int x=1; //local variable
auto int y=2; //automatic variable
}
```

5. External Variable

We can share a variable in multiple C source files by using external variable. To declare an external variable, you need to use extern keyword.

myfile.h
```
extern int x=10; //external variable
```
Let's go through with the whole program :

Program1.c
```
#include<myfile.h>
#include<stdio.h>
void printvalue(){
printf("Global Variable: %d", global_variable);
}
```

Exercise-4

1. Declare a variable of type `int` named `age` and assign it the value 25. Print the value of `age` to the console.

2. Create two variables, `length` and `width`, both of type `float`. Assign the values 5.7 and 3.2 respectively. Calculate the area of a rectangle using these variables and print the result.

3. Declare a variable `character` of type `char` and assign it the value 'A'. Print the character to the console.

4. Declare a variable `isStudent` of type `int` and assign it a value of either 0 or 1 to represent whether a person is a student or not. Print "You are a student" if `isStudent` is 1, and "You are not a student" if `isStudent` is 0.

5. Declare two variables, `num1` and `num2`, both of type `int`. Take input from the user for these two variables using `scanf`, calculate their sum, and print the result.

6. Create a variable `pi` of type `float` and assign it the value 3.14159. Declare another variable `radius` of type `float` and assign it any value of your choice. Calculate the area of a circle using the formula `area = pi * radius * radius` and print the result.

7. Declare a variable `name` of type `char` array with a size of 20. Take input from the user for the name using `scanf` and print a personalized greeting like "Hello, [name]!".

8. Create a variable `count` of type `int` and initialize it with 0. Use a loop to increment the value of `count` by 1, and print its value at each iteration until it reaches 10.

CHAPTER FIVE

Constants and literals in C

Constants refer to fixed values that the program may not alter during its execution. These fixed values are also called literals.

Constants can be of any of the basic data types like an integer constant, a floating constant, a character constant, or a string literal. There are enumeration constants as well.

Constants are treated just like regular variables except that their values cannot be modified after their definition.

Defining Constants:

There are two simple ways in C to define constants -

1. Using #define preprocessor.

2. Using const keyword.

Let us see in detail-

1. The #define Preprocessor

Given below is the form to use #define preprocessor to define a constant

#define identifier value

The following example explains it in detail-

```
#include<stdio.h>
#define LENGTH 10
#define WIDTH 5
#define NEWLINE '/n'
int main(){
int area;
area= LENGTH*WIDTH;
printf("value of area: %d", area);
printf("%c", NEWLINE);
return 0;
}
```

when the above code is compiled and executed, it produces the following result-

value of area : 50

2. The const Keyword

You can use const prefix to declare constants with a specific type follows-

const type variable = value;

Let's see an example to know this in details:

const float PI= 3.14;

Now, the value of PI variable can't be changed.

```
#include<stdio.h>
void main(){
const float PI= 3.14;
printf("The value of PI is: %f" PI);
}
```

Output:

The value of PI is: 3.140000

If you try to change the value of PI, it will render compile time error.

#include<stdio.h>

```
void main(){
const float PI= 3.14;
PI= 4.5;
printf("The value of PI is: %f", PI);
}
```

Output:

Compile Time Error: cannot modify a const object

This is another Example:

```
#include<stdio.h>
int main(){
const int LENGTH= 10;
const int WIDTH= 5;
const int NEWLINE= '\n';
int area;
area= LENGTH * WIDTH;
print("value of area: %d", area);
printf("%c", NEWLINE);
return 0;
}
```

When the above code is compiled and executed, it produces the following **result-**

value of area: 50

NOTE: It is a good programming practice to define constants in CAPITALS

Exercise-5

1. what is Constant in C?
2. what is the differnece between scope and the variable ?
3. write an example for 3 numberic constant in c.
4. what is literals?
5. How are constants stored in memory in C? Explain the memory allocation for different types of constants.
6. How constant and literals impact in C?

CHAPTER SIX

Operator in C

An operator is a symbol that tells the compiler to perform specific mathematical or logical functions. C language is rich in built-in operators and provides the following types of operators -

- Arithmetic Operators
- Relational Operators
- Logical Operators
- Bitwise Operators
- Assignment Operators
- Misc Operators

1.Arithmetic Operators:

The following table shows all the arithmetic operators supported by the C language. Assume variable A holds 10 and variable B holds 20 then-

Operator	Description	Example
+	Adds two operands	A+B=30
-	Subtracts second operand from the first	A-B=-10
*	Multiplies both operands	A*B= 200
/	Divides numerator by de-numerator	B/A=2
%	Modules Operator and reminder of after an Integer Division.	B%A=0
++	Increment Operator increases the integer value by one.	A++= 11
--	Decrement operator decreases the integer value by one.	A--=9

Arithmetic Operator

Here's an example that demonstrates the usage of arithmetic operators in C:

```
#include <stdio.h>
int main() {
int num1 = 10;
int num2 = 5;
int result;
// Addition
result = num1 + num2;
printf("Addition: %d\n", result);
```

```c
   // Subtraction
result = num1 - num2;
printf("Subtraction: %d\n", result);
   // Multiplication
result = num1 * num2;
printf("Multiplication: %d\n", result);
   // Division
result = num1 / num2;
printf("Division: %d\n", result);
   // Modulo (Remainder)
result = num1 % num2;
printf("Modulo: %d\n", result);
   // Increment
num1++;
printf("Increment: %d\n", num1);
   // Decrement
num2--;
printf("Decrement: %d\n", num2);
   return 0;
}
```

Output:

Addition: 15
Subtraction: 5
Multiplication: 50
Division: 2
Modulo: 0
Increment: 11
Decrement: 4

2. Relational Operators:

The following table shows all the relational operators supported by c Assume variable A holds 10 and variable B holds 20 then-

Operator	Description	Example
==	Checks if the values of two operands are equal or not. If yes, then the condition becomes true.	(A==B) is not true
!=	Checks if the values of two operands are equal or not. If the values are not equal, then the condition becomes true.	(A! = B) is true
>	Checks if the value of left operand is greater than the value of right operand. If yes, then the condition becomes true.	(A>B) is not true
<	Checks if the value of left operand is less than the value of right operand. If yes, then the condition becomes true.	(A<B) is true
>=	Checks if the value of left operand is greater than or equal to the value of right operand. If yes, then the condition becomes true.	(A>= B) is not true
<=	Checks if the value of left operand is less than or equal to the value of right operand. If yes, then the condition becomes true	(A<= B) is true

Relational operators

For a better understanding let us see a one example of **Equal to** operator -

```
#include <stdio.h>
   int main() {
int num1 = 45;
int num2 = 7;
   if (num1 == num2) {
printf("num1 is equal to num2\n");
} else {
printf("num1 is not equal to num2\n");
}
   return 0;
}
```

Output:

num1 is not equal to num2

3. Logical Operators:

Following table shows all the logical operators supported by C language. Assume variable A holds 1 and variable B holds 0, then -

Operator	Description	Example
&&	Called Logical AND operator. If both the operands are non-zero, then the condition becomes true.	(A & B) is false.
||	Called Logical OR Operator. If any of the two operands is non-zero, then the condition becomes true.	
!	Called Logical NOT Operator. It is used to reverse the logical state of its operand. If a condition is true, then Logical NOT operator will make it false,	(A && 8) is true.

Logical Operator
Code-

```c
#include <stdio.h>
int main() {
int num = 10;
    // Logical AND (&&)
if (num > 0 && num < 20) {
printf("Number is between 0 and 20.\n");
} else {
printf("Number is outside the range.\n");
}
    // Logical OR (||)
if (num == 0 || num == 10) {
printf("Number is either 0 or 10.\n");
} else {
printf("Number is neither 0 nor 10.\n");
}
    // Logical NOT (!)
if (!(num > 20)) {
printf("Number is not greater than 20.\n");
} else {
printf("Number is greater than 20.\n");
}
    return 0;
}
```

Output:
Number is between 0 and 20.
Number is either 0 or 10.
Number is not greater than 20.

4. Bitwise Operators

Bitwise operator works on bits and perform bit-by-bit operation. The truth tables for 0 &, 1, and A is as follows-

p	q	p&q	p|q	p^q
0	0	0	0	0
0	1	0	1	1
1	1	1	1	0
1	0	0	1	1

Bitwise operators
Assume A 60 and B 13 in binary format, they will be as follows-
A = 0011 3100
B = 0000 1101

A&B = 0000 1100
A|B = 0011 1101
A^B = 0011 0001
~A = 1100 0011

The following table lists the bitwise operators supported by C. Assume variable 'A' holds 60 and variable 'B' holds 13, then

Operator	Description	Example
&	Binary AND Operator copies a bit to the result if it exists in both operands.	(A&B) = 12 i.e., 0000 1100
|	Binary OR Operator copies a bit if it exists in either operand.	(A|B) = 61 i.e., 0011 1101
^	Binary XOR Operator copies the bit if it is set in one operand but not both.	(A^B) = 49 i.e., 0011 0001
~	Binary Ones Complement Operator is unary and has the effect of 'flipping' bits.	(~A) = -61 i.e., 1100 0011 in 2's complement form
<<	Binary Left Shift Operator. The left operands value is moved left by the number of bits specified by the right operand.	A<<2 = 240 i.e., 1111 0000
>>	Binary Right Shift Operator. The left operands value is moved right by the number of bits specified by the right operand.	A>>2 = 15 i.e., 0000 1111

5. Assignment Operators:
The following table lists the assignment operators supported by the C language-

Operator	Description	Example
=	Simple assignment operator. Assigns values from right side operands to left side operand	C = A+B will assign the value of A+ B to C
+=	Add AND assignment operator. It adds the right operand to the left operand and assign the result to the left operand	C+= A is equivalent to C = C+A
-=	Subtract AND assignment operator. It subtracts the right operand from the left operand and assigns the result to the left operand	C-= A is equivalent to C = C- A
*=	Multiply AND assignment operator. It multiplies the right operand with the left operand and assigns the result to the left operand	C*= A is equivalent to C = C * A
/=	Divide AND assignment operator. It divides the left operand with the right operand and assigns the result to the left operand	C/= A IS equivalent to C = C/A
%=	Modulus AND assignment operator. It takes modulus using two operands and assigns the result to the left operand	C%= A is equivalent to C =C%A
<<=	Left shift AND assignment operator	C<<= 2 is same as C = C <<2
>>=	Right shift AND assignment operator.	C >>= 2 is same as C = C >> 2
&=	Bitwise AND assignment operator.	C & = 2 is same as C = C & 2
^=	Bitwise exclusive OR and assignment operator.	CA 2 is same as C = C^2
|=	Bitwise inclusive OR and assignment operator.	C|= 2 is same as C = C	2

Assignment Operator
Example of Assignment Operator;
```
#include <stdio.h>
int main() {
int num1, num2;
num1 = 9; // Assigning the value 10 to num1
num2 = num1; // Assigning the value of num1 to num2
printf("num1: %d\n", num1);
printf("num2: %d\n", num2);
return 0;
}
```
Output:

num1: 9
num2: 9

Misc Operators-sizeof & ternary

Besides the operators discussed above, there are a few other important operators including sizeof and ?: supported by the C Language.

Operator	Description	Example
Sizeof ()	Returns the size of a variable	Sizeof(a), where a is integer, will return 4
&	Returns the address of a variable	&a; returns the actual address of the variable;
*	Pointer to a variable	*a;
?:	Conditional Expression	If Condition is true? The value X: otherwise, value Y

Misc Operators
```
#include <stdio.h>
int main() {
int num = 10;
int arr[] = {1, 3, 5, 7, 9};
    // Example of sizeof operator
int size = sizeof(num);
int sizeArray = sizeof(arr) / sizeof(arr[0]);
    printf("Size of num: %d bytes\n", size);
printf("Size of arr: %d elements\n", sizeArray);
    // Example of ternary operator
int x = 5;
int y = 10;
int max = (x > y) ? x : y;
    printf("Maximum value: %d\n", max);
    return 0;
}
```

Operators Precedence in C

Operator precedence determines the grouping of terms in an expression and decides how an expression is evaluated. Certain operators have higher precedence than others; for example, the multiplication operator has at higher precedence than the addition operator.

For example, x=7+3*2; here, x is assigned 13, not 20 because operator has a higher precedence than, so it first gets multiplied with 3*2 and then adds into 7.

Here, operators with the highest precedence appear at the top of the table, those with the lowest appear at the bottom. Within an expression, higher precedence operators will be evaluated first.

Category	Operator	Associativity
Postfix	() [] -> . ++ --	Left to Right
Unary	+ - ~ ! ++ --(type)* & sizeof	Right to Left
Multiplicative	*/%	Left to Right
Addictive	+ -	Left to Right
Shift	<< >>	Left to Right
Relational	<<= >>=	Left to Right
Equality	= = !=	Left to Right
Bitwise AND	&	Left to Right
Bitwise XOR	^	Left to Right
Bitwise OR	|	Left to Right
Logical AND	&&	Left to Right
Logical OR	||	Left to Right
Conditional	?:	Right to Left
Assignment	=+==-=*=/=%=>>=<<=&=^=|=	Right to Left
Comma	,	Left to Right

Operator Precedence

Exercise -6

1. What is Operator in C?
2. Write a C program to calculate the product of two integers using the multiplication operator (*).
3. Write a C program to increment an integer variable by 1 using the increment operator (++).
4. Write a C program to check if two integers are not equal using the inequality operator (!=).
5. Write a C program to check if one integer is less than or equal to another using the less than or equal to operator (<=).
6. Write a C program to perform a bitwise XOR operation on two integers using the bitwise XOR operator (^).
7. Write a C program to swap the values of two integers without using a temporary variable, using the assignment (=) and arithmetic (+, -) operators.
8. Write a C program to perform a bitwise NOT operation on an integer using the bitwise NOT operator (~).

CHAPTER SEVEN

Control Statement

What Are Control Statements in C?

Control statements are used to control the flow of execution in a program. They allow you to make decisions, repeat a block of code, and alter the normal sequence of statements based on specific conditions. Control statements enable you to create programs that can perform different actions based on input, make decisions, and execute code repeatedly.

Types of Control Statements in C ?

- Decision-making control statements.
- Conditional statements
- Goto statements in C
- Loop control statements in C

Decision-making control statements are:

Decision-making control statements in C are used to make choices and execute specific blocks of code based on certain conditions. The decision-making control statements in C are:

1. if statement:

The if statement is used to execute a block of code if a specified condition is true.

Flow chart:

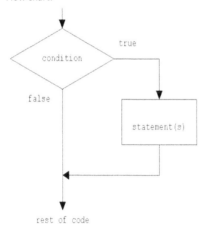

Flow chart of if statement

Syntax:

if (condition)
{
// code to be executed if the condition is true
}

2. if-else statement:

The if-else statement is used to execute one block of code if a condition is true and another block of code if the condition is false.

Syntax:

```
   if (condition)
{
// code to be executed if the condition is true
}
else
{
// code to be executed if the condition is false
}
```

3. nested if-else statement:

The nested if-else statement is used to have multiple if-else statements nested inside each other to handle complex conditions.

Syntax:

```
   if (condition1)
{
// code to be executed if condition1 is true
   if (condition2)
{
// code to be executed if condition2 is true
}
else
{
// code to be executed if condition2 is false
}
}
else
{
// code to be executed if condition1 is false
}
```

Conditional statements are:

1. switch statement:

The switch statement is used to select one of several execution paths based on the value of a variable or an expression.

Syntax:

```
   switch (expression)
{
case value1:
// code to be executed if expression matches value1
break;
case value2:
// code to be executed if expression matches value2
break;
// more cases...
default:
// code to be executed if expression doesn't match any case
break;
}
```

Goto statements in C:

The goto statement allows you to transfer control to a labeled statement within the same function. It provides a way to change the normal flow of execution by directly jumping to a specific point in the code. However, the use of goto is generally discouraged because it can make code harder to understand and maintain. Here is an explanation of the goto statement in C:

Syntax:

goto label;

label: // statement

The goto statement consists of the keyword "goto" followed by a label. The label is a user-defined identifier followed by a colon (":"). The label serves as a marker or target in the code to which control will be transferred.

Example:

```
int main() {
int num = 10;
    if (num > 0) {
goto positive;
}
    printf("Negative number\n");
goto end;
    positive:
printf("Positive number\n");
    end:
printf("End of program\n");
    return 0;
}
```

In the above example, the goto statement is used to transfer control to either the positive label or the end label based on the condition. If num is greater than 0, the control jumps to the positive label and executes the corresponding code. Otherwise, it skips the positive label and continues to execute the code after the goto statement, resulting in printing "Negative number". Finally, the control reaches the end label, and the program exits after printing "End of program".

It is important to use goto judiciously, as excessive or improper use of goto statements can make code difficult to read, understand, and maintain. In most cases, alternative control structures such as loops and conditional statements provide clearer and more maintainable solutions.

Loops

loops are used to repeatedly execute a block of code until a certain condition is met. Loops allow you to automate repetitive tasks and iterate over a set of instructions. There are three types of loops in C: the while loop, the do-while loop, and the for loop.

while loop: The while loop repeatedly executes a block of code as long as a given condition remains true. The condition is evaluated before each iteration.

Flow Chart:

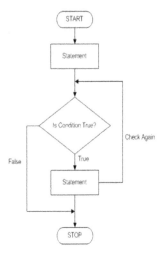

Flow chart of while loop

Syntax:

```
while (condition)
{
// code to be executed
}
```

Example:

```
int i = 1;
while (i <= 5)
{
printf("%d ", i);
i++;
}
```

Output:

1 2 3 4 5

In this example, the while loop prints the value of i from 1 to 5. The loop continues executing as long as the condition i <= 5 remains true. The value of i is incremented by 1 in each iteration.

do-while loop: The do-while loop is similar to the while loop, but it guarantees that the block of code is executed at least once, even if the condition is false. The condition is evaluated after each iteration.

Flow Chart:

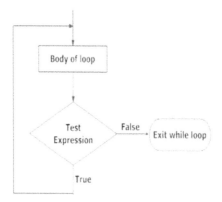

Flow chart of do-while loop

Syntax:

```
do
{
// code to be executed
} while (condition);
```

Example:

```
int i = 1;
do
{
printf("%d ", i);
i++;
} while (i <= 5);
```

Output:

1 2 3 4 5

In this example, the do-while loop behaves similarly to the while loop, but it executes the code block first and then checks the condition. The loop continues as long as the condition i <= 5 remains true.

for loop: The for loop provides a compact way to specify the initialization, condition, and increment/decrement of a loop in a single line. It is commonly used when the number of iterations is known in advance.

Flow Chart:

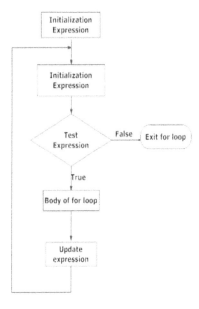

Flow chart of for loop

Syntax:

for (initialization; condition; increment/decrement)
{
// code to be executed
}

Example:

```
for (int i = 1; i <= 5; i++)
{
printf("%d ", i);
}
```

Output:

1 2 3 4 5

In this example, the for loop initializes i to 1, checks the condition i <= 5, executes the code block, and increments i by 1 in each iteration. The loop continues until the condition becomes false.

Loops allow you to efficiently repeat a set of instructions, making your code more concise and eliminating the need for repetitive code. The choice of loop type depends on the specific requirements of your program.

Exercise-7

1. Write a program that accepts an integer input from the user and checks if it is positive, negative, or zero.

2. Write a program that accepts three numbers from the user and prints the largest number using the if-else statement.

3. Write a program that prints all the prime numbers between 1 and 100 using a for loop and if statement.

4. Write a program that calculates the factorial of a given number using a while loop.

5. Write a program that accepts a character from the user and checks if it is a vowel or a consonant using the switch statement.

6. Write a program to find the sum of all even numbers between 1 and 50 using the do-while loop.

7. Write a program that prints the multiplication table of a given number using a for loop.

8. Write a program that accepts a positive integer from the user and checks if it is a perfect number.

9. Write a program that prompts the user to enter a password and allows access only if the correct password is entered (use the if-else statement).

10. Write a program that prints the Fibonacci series up to a given number using the while loop.

CHAPTER EIGHT

Array

Array in C language is a collection or group of elements (data). All the elements of c array are homogeneous (similar). It has contiguous memory location.

C array is beneficial if you have to store similar elements. Suppose you have to store marks of 50 students, one way to do this is allotting 50 variables. So it will be typical and hard to manage. For example we can not access the value of these variables with only 1 or 2 lines of code.

Another way to do this is array. By using array, we can access the elements easily. Only few lines of code is required to access the elements of array.

Advantage of Array

1) Code Optimization: Less code to the access the data.

2) Easy to traverse data: By using the for loop, we can retrieve the elements of an array easily.

3) Easy to sort data: To sort the elements of array, we need a few lines of code only.

4) Random Access: We can access any element randomly using the array.

Disadvantage of Array

1) **Fixed Size:** Whatever size, we define at the time of declaration of array, we can't exceed the limit. So, it doesn't grow the size dynamically like LinkedList which we will learn later.

Declaration of Array

We can declare an array in the c language in the following way.

data_type array_name [array_size];

Now,let us see the example to declare Array.

int marks[5];

here, int is the data_type, marks is the array_name and 5 is the array_size

Initialization Of Array:

A simple way to initialize array is by index.Notice that array index status from 0 and ends with [SIZE - 1]

marks[0]= 80; //initialization of array
marks[1]= 60;
marks[2]=70;
marks[3]=85;
marks[4]=75;

80	60	70	85	75
marks[0]	marks[1]	marks [2]	marks[3]	marks[4]

Initialization of array

Array Example:

```
#include<stdio.h>
int main(){
int -=[];
int marks[5]; //declaration of array
marks[0]= 80; //initialization of array
marks[1]= 60;
```

```
marks[2]=70;
marks[3]=85;
marks[4]=75;
//traversal of array
for(i=0;i<5;i++){
printf("%d \n", marks[i]);
}//end of the for loop
return 0;
}
```

Output:

80
60
70
85
75

Array : Declaration with Initialization

We can initilize the c array at the time of declaration.let's see the code.

int marks[5]= {20,30,40,50,60};

In such case, there is no requirement to define size. So,it can also be written as the following code.

int marks[]={20, 30, 40, 50, 60}

Let's see the **full program** to declare and initialize the array in C.

```
#include<stdio.h>
void main(){
int i=[];
//traversal of array
for(i=0;i<5;i++){
printf("%d \n", marks[i]);
}
}
```

Output:

20
30
40
50
60

Accessing Array Elements:

An elements is asked by indexing the array name. This is done by placing the index of the elements within square brakets after the name of the array.

For Example-

double salary = balance[9];

The above statement will take the 10 element from the array and assi the value to salary variable. The following example Shows how to use all the three above mentioned concepts viz. declaration, assignment, and accessing arrays -

```
#include<stdio.h>
int main(){
int n[10]; /* n is an array of 10 integers */
```

```
/* initilize elements of array n to 0 */
for(i=0;i<10;i++){
n[i] =i+100; /* set element at location i to i+100 */
}
/* output each array elements value */
for(j=0;j<10;j++){
printf("Element[%d]=%d \n", j,n[j]);
}
return 0;
}
```

When the above code is complied and executed , it produces the following **result-**
```
Elelment[0]= 100
Elelment[1]= 101
Elelment[2]= 102
Elelment[3]= 103
Elelment[4]= 104
Elelment[5]= 105
Elelment[6]= 106
Elelment[7]= 107
Elelment[8]= 108
Elelment[9]= 109
```

Single dimensional array

In C, a single-dimensional array is a collection of elements of the same data type arranged in a contiguous block of memory. Each element in the array is accessed using an index, which starts from 0. Here's an example of declaring and using a single-dimensional array in C:

```
#include <stdio.h>

int main() {
// Declare an array of integers with a size of 5
int count[3];

// Assign values to array elements
count[0] = 12;
count[1] = 24;
count[2] = 36;

// Access and print array elements
printf("Element 0: %d\n", count[0]);
printf("Element 1: %d\n", count[1]);
printf("Element 2: %d\n", count[2]);
```

```
    return 0;
}
```

Output:

```
Element 0: 12
Element 1: 24
Element 2: 36
```

In the example above, we declare an array `count` of type `int` with a size of 3. We then assign values to each element using the index notation, starting from 0. Finally, we access and print the elements of the array using the index.

Note that in C, arrays are zero-indexed, meaning the first element is accessed using index 0, the second element with index 1, and so on. The size of the array determines the number of elements it can hold, and once the array is declared, its size cannot be changed.

You can also initialize the array elements during declaration:

```
int count[3] = {12, 24, 36};
```

This initializes the array elements directly with the given values.

Exercise-8

1. what is array in C?
2. List and explain the Types of C.
3. Write a C program to find the sum of all elements in an integer array.
4. Write a C program to find the maximum element in an array.
5. Write a C program to find the minimum element in an array.
6. Write a C program to calculate the average of elements in an array.
7. Write a C program to count the number of even and odd elements in an integer array.
8. Write a C program to reverse the elements in an array.
9. Write a C program to remove duplicate elements from an array.
10. Write a C program to find the second largest element in an array.

CHAPTER NINE

Function

A function is a self-contained block of code that performs a specific task. It provides a way to modularize code and allows you to reuse the same block of code multiple times. Functions are essential for code organization, readability, and maintainability.

Syntax of a Function:

```
return_type function_name(parameter_list) {
// function body (code to be executed)
// optional return statement
}
```

Explanation of the Syntax:

return_type: It specifies the data type of the value that the function returns. It can be void if the function doesn't return any value.

function_name: It is a user-defined name given to the function.

parameter_list: It consists of the data types and names of the parameters (optional) that the function accepts. Multiple parameters are separated by commas.

function body: It contains the code to be executed when the function is called.

return statement: It is an optional statement used to return a value from the function to the calling code.

Types of functions
Types of functions:

C functions are classified into two categories:

1. Standard Library functions

2. User defined functions

Standard Library functions:

Library functions are built-in standard function to perform a certain task. These functions are defined in the header file which needs to be included in the program.

For examples: printf(), scanf(), gets(), puts() etc... are standard library functions.

- **C programming math library functions:**

C standard library provides a huge collection of standard functions for performing various common tasks such as mathematical calculations, input/output, character manipulations, string manipulations etc.

Standard C programming math library functions

We should use C standard library function when possible instead of writing new functions.

C programming math library functions allow us to perform common mathematical computations. For example:

printf("%.2f", sqrt(16));

The above code will calculate square root of 16 using standard sqrt library function. For using this function, we should include math.h header by using preprocessor directive which is shown below:

#include <math.h>

The function arguments can be variables, constant or expressions.
For example: If a=8, b=8

printf("%.2f", sqrt(a + b));

The above statement will calculate and print the square root of a + b.

Commonly used C programming math library functions

sqrt(x)
square root of x

cbrt(x)
cube root of x (C99 and C11 only)

exp(x)
exponential function x

log(x)
natural logarithm of x (base e)

log10(x)
logarithm of x (base 10)

fabs(x)
absolute value of x as a floating-point

ceil(x)
rounds x to the smallest integer not less than x

floor(x)
rounds x to the largest integer not greater than x

pow(x, y)
x raised to power y (xy)

fmod(x, y)
remainder of x/y as a floating-point number

sin(x)
trigonometric sine of x

cos(x)
trigonometric cosine of x

tan(x)
trigonometric tangent of x

User defined functions:

The user defined functions are written by a programmer at the time of writing the program. When the function is called, the execution of the program is shifted to the first statement of called function.

Function declaration in c:

A function declaration is a statement that informs the compiler about the name, return type, and parameters of a function before its actual definition. It acts as a contract or prototype for the function, providing information about how the function should be called and used in the program. Function declarations are typically placed at the beginning of the program or in header files.

Here's the syntax for function declaration in C:

return_type function_name(parameter_list);

Explanation of the Syntax:

- return_type: It specifies the data type of the value that the function returns. It can be any valid C data type, including void if the function doesn't return any value.
- function_name: It is the name of the function that you are declaring. Choose a descriptive name that reflects the purpose of the function.
- parameter_list: It consists of the data types and names of the parameters (optional) that the function accepts. Multiple parameters are separated by commas.

Example of Function Declaration:

#include <stdio.h>

```
// Function declaration
int addNumbers(int a, int b);

int main() {
int num1 = 10, num2 = 20;
int sum = addNumbers(num1, num2);
printf("Sum: %d\n", sum);
return 0;
}

// Function definition
int addNumbers(int a, int b) {
return a + b;
}
```

In the above example, the function addNumbers is declared at the beginning of the program before the main function. The declaration specifies the return type int and the parameter list (int a, int b). This allows the main function to call addNumbers and pass the required arguments.

Function declarations are essential when functions are defined after their first use in the program. By declaring the functions beforehand, the compiler knows about the existence, return type, and parameter types of the function, which allows it to perform proper type checking and ensure correct usage of the function.

Function declarations are often placed in header files (.h) so that they can be shared across multiple source files in a program or between different programs. This helps in modularizing the code and promoting code reuse.

Function definition in c:

A function definition is a block of code that specifies the actual implementation or body of a function. It contains the instructions that are executed when the function is called. The function definition provides the details of how the function performs its task.

Here's the syntax for function definition in C:

```
return_type function_name(parameter_list) {
// function body (code to be executed)
// optional return statement
}
```

Explanation of the Syntax:

- return_type: It specifies the data type of the value that the function returns. It can be any valid C data type, including void if the function doesn't return any value.

- function_name: It is the name of the function that you are defining. The name should match the function name used in the declaration and any function calls.
- parameter_list: It consists of the data types and names of the parameters (optional) that the function accepts. Multiple parameters are separated by commas.
- function body: It contains the actual code that is executed when the function is called. It can include variable declarations, statements, loops, conditionals, and other control structures.
- return statement: It is an optional statement used to return a value from the function to the calling code. It is specified using the return keyword followed by an expression or a variable.

Example of Function Definition:

```
#include <stdio.h>

// Function declaration
int addNumbers(int a, int b);

int main() {
int num1 = 10, num2 = 20;
int sum = addNumbers(num1, num2);
printf("Sum: %d\n", sum);
return 0;
}

// Function definition
int addNumbers(int a, int b) {
int result = a + b;
return result;
}
```

In the above example, the function addNumbers is defined after the main function. The function definition specifies the return type int, the function name addNumbers, and the parameter list (int a, int b). Inside the function body, the sum of the two parameters is calculated and stored in the result variable. Finally, the result is returned using the return statement.

Function definitions provide the actual implementation of the function and determine how the function behaves when called. They should match the declaration in terms of return type, function name, and parameter types. By separating the function declaration and definition, you can modularize your code and reuse functions in different parts of the program.

Function calling in c:

Function calling refers to the process of invoking or executing a function from another part of the program. When a function is called, the program transfers control to that function, and the function executes its defined set of instructions. Here's how you can call a function in C:

Syntax for Function Calling:

return_type function_name(argument_list);

Explanation of the Syntax:

return_type: It is the data type of the value that the function returns. It can be any valid C data type, including void if the function doesn't return any value.

function_name: It is the name of the function that you want to call.

argument_list: It consists of the values or expressions (optional) that are passed as arguments to the function. Multiple arguments are separated by commas.

Example of Function Calling:

```c
#include <stdio.h>

// Function declaration
int addNumbers(int a, int b);

int main() {
int num1 = 10, num2 = 20;
int sum = addNumbers(num1, num2); // Function call
printf("Sum: %d\n", sum);
return 0;
}

// Function definition
int addNumbers(int a, int b) {
int result = a + b;
return result;
}
```

In the above example, the function addNumbers is called from the main function using the statement addNumbers(num1, num2). The values of num1 and num2 are passed as arguments to the function. The function is executed, and the returned value is assigned to the sum variable.

When the function call is encountered, the program transfers control to the called function. The called function executes its defined set of instructions. In this case, the addNumbers function calculates the sum of two numbers and returns the result. The control then returns to the point of function call in the main function.

It's important to note that the function being called should be declared or defined before the point of the function call. This ensures that the compiler knows about the function's existence, return type, and parameter types, enabling proper type checking and correct usage of the function.

Return type in function:

the return type in a function specifies the data type of the value that the function returns to the calling code. It indicates the type of the result or output that the function provides after performing its task. The return type is declared in the function declaration and definition. Here's an explanation of return types in functions in C:

1. Returning a Value:

If a function is expected to return a value, the return type should be specified as a valid C data type (e.g., int, float, char, etc.).

The function must use a return statement to send the result back to the calling code.

The return statement typically includes an expression or a variable of the declared return type.

Example:

```
int addNumbers(int a, int b) {
int sum = a + b;
return sum;
}
```

2. Void Return Type:

If a function does not need to return a value, the return type should be specified as void.

The function does not need to include a return statement, or it can have a return statement without any expression.

Example:

```
void greet() {
printf("Hello, World!\n");
// No return statement or return statement without an expression
}
```

3. Returning a Pointer:

A function can also return a pointer to a memory location or an object.

The return type should be specified as the corresponding pointer type.

Example:

```
int* createArray(int size) {
int* arr = malloc(size * sizeof(int));
// Perform some operations on the array
return arr;
}
```

It's important to note that the return type declared in the function declaration and definition must match. The calling code expects the function to return a value of the specified type. If the function does not return a value when it should, or returns a value of a different type, it can lead to undefined behavior or compilation errors.

The choice of return type depends on the purpose of the function and the type of result it should provide to the calling code. Functions can be designed to perform calculations, modify variables, manipulate data structures, or carry out specific tasks. The return type allows the function to communicate the result of its operation back to the calling code.

Pass by value:

passing arguments to a function can be done by value or by reference. When passing arguments by value, the value of the arguments is copied and provided to the function. Any modifications made to the arguments inside the function do not affect the original variables in the calling code. Here's an explanation of pass by value in C:

Pass by Value:

In pass by value, the values of the arguments are passed to the function as copies.

The function works with these copies of the arguments.

Any changes made to the copies inside the function do not affect the original variables in the calling code.

Example:

```
void increment(int num) {
num = num + 1; // Increment the copy of num
printf("Inside the function: %d\n", num);
}

int main() {
int num = 10;
increment(num); // Pass the value of num to the function
```

```
printf("In the main function: %d\n", num);
return 0;
}
```

Output:
Inside the function: 11
In the main function: 10

In the example above, the function increment takes an argument num by value. It increments the copy of num inside the function. However, the original variable num in the main function remains unchanged.

Pass by value is the default method of passing arguments in C. It is suitable when you want to work with a local copy of the arguments without modifying the original variables.

For passing more complex data structures, like arrays or structures, pass by value still creates a copy of the entire data structure, which can be inefficient for large data.

If you want to modify the original variables in the calling code, you need to use pass by reference, which involves passing the addresses of the variables to the function using pointers.

Pass by reference:

pass by reference allows you to pass arguments to a function by providing the addresses of the variables. By passing arguments by reference, any modifications made to the arguments inside the function will affect the original variables in the calling code. Here's an explanation of pass by reference in C:

Pass by Reference:

In pass by reference, the addresses (pointers) of the arguments are passed to the function.

The function can access and modify the values of the original variables through these pointers.

Any changes made to the variables inside the function will directly affect the original variables in the calling code.

Example:

```
void increment(int* ptr) {
(*ptr)++; // Increment the value at the address pointed by ptr
}

int main() {
int num = 10;
increment(&num); // Pass the address of num to the function
```

```
printf("In the main function: %d\n", num);
return 0;
}
```

Output:

In the main function: 11

In the example above, the function increment takes a pointer argument ptr. It increments the value at the address pointed by ptr using the dereference operator *. By passing the address of the variable num to the function using &num, the original variable num in the main function is modified.

Pass by reference is useful when you want to modify the original variables in the calling code or when you want to avoid making copies of large data structures like arrays or structures.

In addition to pointers, pass by reference can also be achieved in C++ using references, but it is not a native feature in standard C.

It's important to note that when using pass by reference, you need to ensure that the function declaration includes the correct pointer type for the argument, and you need to properly dereference the pointer inside the function to access and modify the value.

Pass by reference can be more efficient than pass by value when working with large data structures since it avoids the overhead of copying the entire data structure.

Multi-dimensional array

In C, a multi-dimensional array is an array with two or more dimensions. It is essentially an array of arrays. Here's an example of how to declare, initialize, and access elements in a multi-dimensional array:

```
#include <stdio.h>

int main() {
int matrix[3][3]; // Declaration of a 3x3 multi-dimensional array

// Initialization of the multi-dimensional array
matrix[0][0] = 1;
matrix[0][1] = 3;
matrix[0][2] = 5;
matrix[1][0] = 7;
matrix[1][1] = 9;
matrix[1][2] = 11;

// Accessing and printing elements of the multi-dimensional array
for (int i = 0; i < 3; i++) {
for (int j = 0; j < 3; j++) {
```

```
        printf("%d ", matrix[i][j]);
    }
    printf("\n");
}

return 0;
}
```

Output:

```
1 3 5
7 9 11
```

In the example above, we declare a 3x2 multi-dimensional array named `matrix`. We then initialize the elements of the array with values . Finally, we use nested loops to access and print the elements of the multi-dimensional array.

You can modify the size of the array and assign values to the elements based on your specific requirements.

Exercise-9

1. Write a program to find the maximum between two numbers using a function.

2. Write a program to check if a given number is prime or not using a function.

3. Write a program to calculate the factorial of a given number using a recursive function.

4. Write a program to swap the values of two variables using a function.

5. Write a program to find the sum of all elements in an array using a function.

6. Write a program to reverse a string using a function.

7. Write a program to calculate the area of a circle using a function.

8. Write a program to find the LCM (Least Common Multiple) of two numbers using a function.

9. Write a program to check if a given string is a palindrome using a function.

10. Write a program to convert a decimal number to binary using a function.

CHAPTER TEN

String

A string is a sequence of characters which is treated as a single data item in C. It can also be said an array of characters and any group of characters defined between double quotations is string constants.

"trytoprogram" is an example of string

Now, try2program is a string with a group of 11 characters.

Each character occupies 1 byte of memory.

These characters are placed in consecutive memory locations; after all, string is an array of characters.

address of "t" = 1000 (say)
address of "r" = 1001
address of "y" = 1002
address of "2" = 1003
address of "p" = 1004
address of "r" = 1005
address of "o" = 1006
address of "g" = 1007
address of "r" = 1008
address of "a" = 1009
address of "m" = 1010

String and memory:

As we know string is the sequence of arrays and is placed in consecutive memory locations.

To indicate the termination of string a null character is always placed at the end of the string in the memory. Now above string will be stored in memory location like this:

1000	1001	1002	1003	1004	1005	1006	1007	1008	1009	1010	1011
T	R	Y	2	P	R	O	G	R	A	M	\o

Declaring and Initializing string variables:

String is not a data type in C, so character arrays are used to represent strings in C and are declared as:

char string_name [size];

The length of a string is always greater than the number of string characters by one because when a compiler assigns a character string to a character array, it automatically supplies a null character ('\o') at the end of the string.

Initializing string arrays:

Strings in C can be initialized in following ways:

char string_name [12] = "try2program";
char string_name [12] = {'t','r','y','2','p','r','o','g','r','a','m','\0'};

In the above example, the size of an array will be determined automatically by the compiler.

Note: Difference between 0, '0', '\0', "0".

0 //an integer value

'0' //character value

'\0' //an escape sequence representing null character

"0" //string representation

How to read strings from users?

Basically, there are two ways for reading the string from users:

    using scanf function

    using getchar and gets functions

using scanf function:

The method of reading string using input function scanf with %s format specifications is the most infamous method.

However, with this scanf function, we can only read a word because this function terminates its input on the first white space it encounters.

For example:

char name [10];

scanf("%s", name);

Note: Normally, an ampersand is used before scanf function while reading the value of variables but in the case of character arrays, we don't need an ampersand (&) because string name itself acts as a pointer to the first variable location.

using getchar and gets functions:

scanf function is used to read only a word and to read a whole line of text either getchar or gets function is used.

This function can be used to read successive single characters from the input until a new line character '\n' is encountered and then null character is inserted at the end of the string.

Syntax of getchar function

char name;

name = getchar( );

Note: getchar function has no parameters.

Syntax of gets function

char name;

getchar(name);

String manipulations

string manipulation refers to performing various operations on strings such as copying, concatenating, comparing, searching, and modifying strings. These operations can be achieved using string manipulation functions provided by the standard library <string.h>.

Some of the major string handling functions used are tabulated below.

Function	Work
Strcat()	Concatenates two strings
Strlen()	Finds the length of string
Strcpy()	Copies one string in to another string
Strcmp()	Compares two strings
Strlwr()	Converts string to lowercase
Strupr()	Converts string to uppercase
Strstr()	Finds first occurrence of substring in string
Strtok()	Splits strings into tokens

Function strcpy copies its second argument into its first argument and we must ensure that array is large enough to store strings of second arguments and a null character.

Function strcmp compares its first and second arguments character wise. It returns 0 if the strings are equal.
It returns a positive value if the first string is greater than second.
It returns a negative value if the first string is less than second.

Function strlen returns the length of input string. It does not include a null character in the length of the string.

puts( ) and putchar( ) function:

This both function are defined in input/output library stdio.h and are used for manipulating string and character data.

Syntax of putchar:

int putchar(int x);

This will print the character stored in x and returns it as an integer.

Syntax of puts:

puts("\nHello World!!!");

This will print "Hello World!!!".

Exercise-10

1. Write a program to find the length of a string without using the built-in string functions.

2. Write a program to concatenate two strings without using the built-in string functions.

3. Write a program to count the number of vowels in a given string.

4. Write a program to reverse a given string.

5. Write a program to check if a given string is a palindrome.

6. Write a program to convert all lowercase characters in a string to uppercase.

7. Write a program to count the occurrence of a specific character in a given string.

8. Write a program to find the frequency of each character in a string and display the result.

9. Write a program to remove all the spaces from a given string.

10. Write a program to check if two strings are anagrams of each other.

CHAPTER ELEVEN

Recursion

Recursion in C refers to a programming technique in which a function calls itself within its own definition. It is a process of solving a problem by breaking it down into smaller, simpler instances of the same problem until a base case is reached. The base case defines the terminating condition that stops the recursive calls, while the recursive case defines the logic to break down the problem into smaller subproblems and call the function recursively.

Here's an example of a simple recursive function in C to calculate the factorial of a number:

```c
#include <stdio.h>
int factorial(int n) {
// Base case: factorial of 0 or 1 is 1
if (n == 0 || n == 1) {
return 1;
}
else {
// Recursive case: n! = n * (n-1)!
return n * factorial(n - 1);
}
}
    int main() {
int number;
printf("Enter a non-negative integer: ");
scanf("%d", &number);

if (number < 0) {
printf("Factorial is not defined for negative numbers.\n");
}
else {
int result = factorial(number);
printf("Factorial of %d is %d\n", number, result);
}

return 0;
}
```

In this example, the factorial function takes an integer n as an argument and calculates the factorial of that number using recursion. It checks for the base case (when n is 0 or 1) and returns 1. Otherwise, it recursively calls itself with n-1 and multiplies the result by n.

When you run the program, it prompts the user to enter a non-negative integer and calculates its factorial using the recursive factorial function.

It's important to note that when working with recursive functions, you must ensure that there is a well-defined base case to avoid infinite recursion.

Exercise-11

1. Write a program to calculate the factorial of a given number using recursion.

2. Write a program to find the nth Fibonacci number using recursion.

3. Write a program to calculate the sum of digits in a given number using recursion.

4. Write a program to reverse a string using recursion.

5. Write a program to check if a given string is a palindrome using recursion.

6. Write a program to find the GCD (Greatest Common Divisor) of two numbers using recursion.

7. Write a program to calculate the power of a number using recursion.

8. Write a program to print all possible permutations of a given string using recursion.

9. Write a program to find the sum of all elements in an array using recursion.

10. Write a program to solve the Tower of Hanoi problem using recursion.

CHAPTER TWELVE
Pointer in C

What are Pointers?

A pointer is a variable that is the direct address of a memory location whose value is the address of
another variable. As with any variable or constant, you must declare a pointer before using it to store the address of any variable. The general form of the pointer variable declared –

Type *variable_name;

where type is the root type of the pointer; must be a valid C file and var-name is the name of the pointer variable. The asterisk used to declare a pointer is the same as that used for equality. However, in this section the asterisk is used to identify the variable as a pointer.

Check out some helpful ads –

int *ip ; /*pointer of integer */
double *dp; /*pointer of double*/
float *fp ; /* pointer of float*/
char *ch; /* pointer of character*/

The actual data value of any integer, floating point, symbol, or other pointer is the same; is a long hexadecimal number representing a memory address. The difference between pointers to a data variable is the data type of the variable or constant to the pointer to the pointer.

How to use Pointers?

There are some important tasks that most of us use pointers to complete.

a.   We define the pointer variable,
b.   We assign the address of the variable to the pointer, and
c.   Finally, we enter the value of theaddress contained in the pointer variable replacement.

This is done using the unary operator *, which returns the value of the variable at the address specified by its operand.

This programming example uses this function –

```
#include<stdio.h>
int main (){
int var =20; /* actual variable declaration */
int *ip; /* pointer variable declaration*/
ip= &var /* store address of var in pointer variable */
printf(" Address store in var variable: %x\n", &var);
/* address stored in pointer variable */
Printf(" Address stored In ip variable: %x\n", ip);
/* access the value using the pointer */
Printf("value of *ip variable: %d\n", *ip);
Return 0;
}
```

When the above code is complied and executed, it produces the followi result -
Address of var variable: bffd9b6c
Address stored in ip variable: bffd9b6c
Value of *ip variable : 20

Types of Pointer

NULL Pointer :

It is always a good practice to assign a NULL value to a pointer variable in case you do not have an exact address to be assigned. This is done at the time of variable declaration. A pointer that is assigned NULL is called a null pointer.

The NULL pointer is a constant with a value of zero defined in several standard libraries. Consider the following program -

```
#include<stdio.h>

int main(){

int *ptr = NULL;

printf("The value of ptr is: %x\n", ptr);

return 0;

}
```

When the above code is compiled and executed, it produces the following result-

The valye if ptr is : 0

In most operating systems, memory at address o is reserved by the operating system, so programs are not allowed to access memory at address o. But the memory address o has a special meaning. This indicates that the pointer cannot be accessed to point to a memory location. However, by convention, a pointer is considered to point to nothing if it contains the value zero (zero).

To check for a null pointer, you can use an 'if' statement as follows -

if(ptr) /* suceeds if p is not null */

if(!ptr) /* suceeds if p is null */

- **Void Pointer :**

A void pointer, denoted by the symbol "void *", is a generic pointer type that can point to an object of any type. However, since it's a public type, you can't directly modify void pointers or perform pointer arithmetic on them. Must be explicitly cast to a specific pointer type before use.

Let us see by observing Code-

```c
#include <stdio.h>

void pointer(void *ptr, char type) {
switch (type) {

case 'x':
printf("Value: %d\n", *((int *)ptr));
break;

case 'y':
printf("Value: %f\n", *((float *)ptr));
break;

default:
printf("Invalid type\n");
break;
}
}

int main() {
int num = 13;
float pi = 3.14159;

printValue(&num, 'a'); // Passing an integer value
printValue(&pi, 'g'); // Passing a float value

return 0;
}
```

Output:

Value: 10
Value: 3.140000

- **Function Pointer :**

A function pointer is a pointer that points to a function instead of a variable. Function pointers are used to store the address of a function, which allows for indirect function calling and dynamic linking of functions.

```c
#include <stdio.h>
```

```
int add(int a, int b) {
return a + b;
}

int main() {
int a = 12;
int b = 3;
int result;

// Declaration of function pointer
int (*operation)(int, int);

// Assigning the address of the function to the pointer
operation = add;
result = operation(a, b);
printf("Addition: %d\n", result);

return 0;
}
```

Output:

Addition: 15

- **Pointer to array:**

A pointer can also be used to store the address of an array. If the pointer points to the first element of the array, it can be traversed using pointer arithmetic. for more clarification let's see a code-

```
#include <stdio.h>

int main() {
int arr[5] = {11, 22, 33, 44, 55};
int *ptr = arr; // Pointer to the first element of the array

printf("Array elements using pointer:\n");
for (int i = 0; i < 5; i++) {
printf("Element %d: %d\n", i, *(ptr + i));
}

return 0;
}
```

Output:

Array elements using pointer:
Element 0: 11

Element 1: 22
Element 2: 33
Element 3: 44
Element 4: 55

- **A pointer to a structure:**

You can use pointers to refer to structures, so you can indirectly access and modify the members of the structure.

Code-

```
#include <stdio.h>
#include <string.h>

struct man {
char name[50];
int age;
};

int main() {
struct Person person; // Declare a structure variable
struct Person *ptr = &man; // Declare a pointer to the structure variable

// Access and modify structure members using the arrow operator ->
strcpy(ptr->name, "Ram");
ptr->age = 23;

// Display the structure members using the pointer
printf("Name: %s\n", ptr->name);
printf("Age: %d\n", ptr->age);

return 0;
}
```

Output:

Name: Ram
Age: 23

Call By Value and Call By Reference

In the C programming language, there are two different ways to pass arguments to functions: **Call by value and Call by reference**. These methods determine how the function receives and manipulates the passed values.

1. Call by Value :
When a function is called with an argument passed by value, the function receives a copy

of the argument's value. Changes made to the parameters inside the function do not affect the original values passed by the caller.

Here's an example that shows a call by value:

```
#include <stdio.h>

void callbyvalue(int num) {
num = 150;
}

int main() {
int num = 15;
printf("Before function call: %d\n", num);
changeValue(num);
printf("After function call: %d\n", num);
return 0;
}
```

Output:

Before function call: 15
After function call: 15

In the example above, the 'callbyvalue' function takes the integer argument 'num' as its value. If you call 'callbyvalue' with 'num' as an argument, you will get a copy of the value '15'. This function changes the copied value to '150'. However, this change does not affect the original num variable in the main function. So the value does not change.

2. Call by Reference :
When a function is called with an argument passed by reference, the function receives a reference to the memory location of the argument. Changes made to the parameters inside the function affect the original values passed by the caller.

Here's an example that shows a call by reference:

```
#include <stdio.h>

void callbyreference(int *num) {
*num = 150;
}

int main() {
int num = 15;
printf("Before function call: %d\n", num);
changeValue(&num);
printf("After function call: %d\n", num);
```

```
    return 0;
}
```

Output:

Before function call: 15
After function call: 150

In this example, the "callbyreference" function receives a pointer to an integer as an argument. Inside the function, the value in the memory location pointed to by "num" is changed to "150". Since we passed the address of the 'num' variable using the '&' operator from the 'main' function, the change is reflected in the main 'num' variable whose value is '150'.

In short, a call by value passes a copy of the value to the function, while a call by reference passes the memory address of the variable, allowing the function to modify the original value.

Exercise-12

1. what is pointer and it's type?
2. What is Call by Value and Call by reference ?
3. Write a program that concatenates two strings using pointers.
4. what is the use of pointer in C?
5. Write a program that dynamically allocates memory for an integer array of size n and then reads n integers from the user. Print the sum and average of these numbers using pointers.
6. Write a program to calculate the factorial of a given number.
7. Implement a program to check whether a given number is prime or not
8. Write a program to find the sum of all elements in an array.
9. Implement a program to reverse a string without using any library functions.
10. Write a program to find the largest and smallest elements in an array.

CHAPTER THIRTEEN

Type casting in C

Type casting allows us to convert one data type into other. In C language, we use cast operator for type casting which is denoted by (type).

Syntax:

{type}value;

Note: It is recommended to always typecast from lower value to higher in order to avoid data loss.

Without Type Casting:

int f=9/4;

printf("f: %d\n",f);//output:2

With Type Casting:

float f={float}9/4;

printf("f: %f\n", f); //output: 2.250000

Let's see a simple example to cast int value into float

#include<stdio.h>

void main(){

float F={float}9/4;

printf("F: %f \n", f);

}

Output:

F: 2.250000

Exercise-13

1. what is the impotance of type casting in C
2. Develop a C program that reads a floating-point number from the user and rounds it to the nearest integer using type casting. Display the rounded integer value.
3. Write a C program that calculates the area of a circle. Prompt the user to enter the radius (a floating-point number) and display the area as a floating-point value using type casting.

CHAPTER FOURTEEN

Union

A union is a special data type available in C that allows different data types to be stored in the same memory location. A union can be defined with many members, but only one member can contain a value at a time. Unions provide an efficient way to use a memory location for multiple purposes.

Definition of union

To define a union, you must use the Union statement in the same way you would define a structure. A union statement defines a new data type with multiple members in the program. The statement of the union is as follows:

union[union tag]{
member defination;
member defination;
...
member defination;
}[one or more union variables];

The union tag is optional, and each member definition is a normal variable definition, such as int i; or float f; or any other valid variable definition. At the end of the union definition, before the last semicolon, you can specify one or more union variables, but this is optional. Here is how you would define a union type called Data with three members a, g and str-

union Set{
int a;
int g ;
char str[30];
} set;

A variable of type Data can now store an integer, a floating-point number, or a character string. This means that one variable, i.e. the same location in memory, can be used to store multiple types of data. You can use any built-in or user-defined data types in the union based on your requirement.

The memory occupied by the union will be large enough to accommodate the largest member of the union. For example, in the above example, the data type will occupy 20 bytes of memory space, because this is the maximum space that a character string can occupy. The following example shows the total memory size occupied by the above union −

```
#include<stdio.h>
#include<string.h>
union Set{
int a;
int g ;
char str[30];
};
int main( ){
union Set set;
printf(" Memory size Occupied ; %d\n", sizeof(set));
return 0;
```

}
When the above code is complied and executed, it produces the following output:
Memory size Occupied : 30;

Accessing Union Members

To access any member of a union, we use the member access operator (.). The member access operator is coded as a period between the union variable name and the union member that we wish to access. You would use the keyword union to define variables of union type. The following example shows how to use unions in a program -

```
#include<stdio.h>
#include<string.h>
union Set{
int a;
int g ;
char str[30];
};
int main( ){
union Set set;
set.a=11;
set.g= 220.5;
printf(set.str, "Programming Language C ");
printf(" set.a : %d\n", data.a);
printf(" set.g : %d\n", data.g);
printf(" set.str : %s\n", data.str);
return 0;
}
```

When the above code is compiled and executed, it produces the following result-
set.a= 1917853768
set.g= 41223605803277948604452759994.00000
set.str= Programming Language C

Here we see that the values of members a and g of the union are corrupted because the final values assigned to the variables have occupied memory locations. This is why the value of the str member prints out so nicely.

Now let's look at the same example again. Here we use one variable at a time. This is the main purpose of having a union.

```
#include<stdio.h>
#include<string.h>
union Set{
int a;
int g ;
char str[30];
};
int main(){
union Set set;
set.a=10;
printf(" set.a : %d\n", data.a);
set.g= 220.5;
printf(" set.g : %d\n", data.g);
```

```
strpy(set.str," Programming Language C")
printf(" set.str : %s\n", data.str);
return 0;
}
```
Output of the code will be -
set.a= 10
set.g= 220.500000
set.str= Programming Language C

Here, all the members are getting printed very well because one member is being used at a time.

Exercise-14

1. What is union in C?
2. Define a union named "Shape" that can represent Square. The Square should have members for sides. Write a program to demonstrate the usage of this union.
3. Define a union named "Book" that can represent either a paperback book or a hardcover book. The paperback book should have members for title, author, and price, while the hardcover book should have members for title, author, and edition. Write a program to demonstrate the usage of this union and display the details of a book based on the user's choice.

CHAPTER FIFTEEN

File Handling in C

File handling in C involves reading data from files and writing data to files. It allows you to perform various operations on files such as creating, opening, reading, writing, appending, and closing files. The C programming language provides several built-in functions and libraries to handle file operations.

Here's a step-by-step guide on file handling in C:

1. Include the necessary header file: To use file handling functions in C, you need to include the <stdio.h> header file, which contains the required functions and definitions.

#include <stdio.h>

2. Declare a file pointer variable: In C, you need to declare a file pointer variable that will be used to point to the file you want to operate on. The file pointer is used to perform operations on files, such as opening, reading, or writing.

FILE *filePointer;

3. Open a file: Before performing any operation on a file, you need to open it using the fopen() function. The fopen() function takes two parameters: the name of the file and the mode in which you want to open it (read, write, append, etc.). The function returns a pointer to the file if the operation is successful, or NULL if there is an error.

filePointer = fopen("filename.txt", "mode");

Here, "filename.txt" is the name of the file you want to open, and "mode" specifies the purpose for which you are opening the file. For example:

"r": Opens the file in read mode.

"w": Opens the file in write mode. If the file already exists, it truncates its content. If the file doesn't exist, it creates a new file.

"a": Opens the file in append mode. If the file already exists, it appends new data at the end. If the file doesn't exist, it creates a new file.

4. Perform file operations: Once the file is successfully opened, you can perform various operations on it. Here are some commonly used file operations:

Reading from a file: To read data from a file, you can use functions like fscanf() or fgets(). The fscanf() function reads formatted data from the file, while the fgets() function reads a line of text from the file.

char buffer[100];
fscanf(filePointer, "%s", buffer); // Read a word from the file
fgets(buffer, sizeof(buffer), filePointer); // Read a line from the file

- Writing to a file: To write data to a file, you can use functions like fprintf() or fputs(). The fprintf() function writes formatted data to the file, while the fputs() function writes a string to the file.

fprintf(filePointer, "%d", 42); // Write an integer to the file
fputs("Hello, World!", filePointer); // Write a string to the file

- Closing a file: Once you are done performing operations on a file, it's important to close it using the fclose() function. Closing a file frees up system resources and ensures that the file is properly saved.

fclose(filePointer);

5. Error handling: When working with files, it's essential to handle errors that may occur during file operations. You can check the return value of functions like fopen() to determine if the file was successfully opened or not. If the file pointer returned by fopen() is NULL, it

indicates that there was an error opening the file. You can use conditional statements to handle such errors and display appropriate error messages.

Here's an example that demonstrates basic file handling operations in C:

```c
#include <stdio.h>
int main() {
FILE *filePointer;
char buffer[100];
    // Open the file in write mode
filePointer = fopen("file.txt", "w");
if (filePointer == NULL) {
printf("Error opening the file.\n");
return 1;
}
    // Write data to the file
fprintf(filePointer, "Hello, World!\n");
fputs("This is a test.", filePointer);
    // Close the file
fclose(filePointer);
    // Open the file in read mode
filePointer = fopen("file.txt", "r");
if (filePointer == NULL) {
printf("Error opening the file.\n");
return 1;
}
    // Read data from the file
fscanf(filePointer, "%s", buffer);
printf("Data from file: %s\n", buffer);
    // Close the file
fclose(filePointer);
    return 0;
}
```

In this example, the program opens a file named "file.txt" in write mode, writes some data to it, and then closes the file. Next, it opens the same file in read mode, reads data from it, and displays the read data on the console. Finally, it closes the file again.

It's important to note that file handling operations may vary depending on the specific requirements of your program. You can explore additional file handling functions available in the <stdio.h> header file, such as feof(), rewind(), and fseek(), to perform more advanced file operations in C.

Exercise-15

1. Write a program that creates a text file and writes "Hello, World!" to it.

2. Write a program that reads a text file and displays its content on the console.

3. Write a program that appends a new line of text to an existing text file.

4. Write a program that counts the number of characters, words, and lines in a text file.

5. Write a program that copies the contents of one text file to another.

6. Write a program that searches for a specific word in a text file and displays the line numbers where the word is found.

7. Write a program that reads a binary file containing student records and displays the average marks of all students.

8. Write a program that encrypts the contents of a text file using a simple encryption algorithm.

9. Write a program that reads a CSV file containing student names and their respective marks and calculates the average marks for each student.

10. Write a program that deletes a specific line from a text file and creates a new file without the deleted line.

CHAPTER SIXTEEN

Dynamic Memory Allocation

Dynamic memory allocation also called as **DMA** allows programs to dynamically allocate memory at runtime. This allows you to allocate and distribute memory based on the needs of your application. C provides four main functions for dynamic memory allocation: 'malloc', 'calloc', 'realloc' and 'free'.

"calloc()" and "free()" functions:

The 'calloc' function is used to allocate a block of memory and initialize it to zero. It takes two parameters: the number of elements to allocate and the size of each element. The total allocated memory will be "(number of elements * size of each element)". A successful allocation returns a pointer to the allocated memory. An example is shown below.

```c
    #include <stdio.h>
#include <stdlib.h>
    int main() {
int *ptr;
int elements = 6;
    ptr = (int *)calloc(elements, sizeof(int));
if (ptr == NULL) {
printf("Memory allocation failed!\n");
exit(1);
}
    // Use the allocated memory
for (int i = 0; i < elements; i++) {
ptr[i] = i + 1;
printf("%d ", ptr[i]);
}
    // Free the allocated memory
free(ptr);
    return 0;
}
    Output:
    1 2 3 4 5 6
```

The above example uses calloc to allocate memory for an array of 6 integers. It then allocates the value in the allocated memory and prints it. Finally, use the "free" function to free the allocated memory.

realloc() and free() functions:

The realloc function is used to change the size of an already allocated block of memory. It takes two parameters: a pointer to an already allocated block of memory and the new size in bytes. A successful reallocation returns a pointer to the newly allocated memory. An example is shown below.

```c
    #include <stdio.h>
#include <stdlib.h>
```

```c
    int main() {
int *ptr;
int elements = 6;
    ptr = (int *)malloc(elements * sizeof(int));
if (ptr == NULL) {
printf("Memory allocation failed!\n");
exit(1);
}
    // Use the allocated memory
for (int i = 0; i < elements; i++) {
ptr[i] = i + 1;
printf("%d ", ptr[i]);
}
    // Reallocate the memory to store 10 elements
int elements = 10;
ptr = (int *)realloc(ptr, newelements * sizeof(int));
if (ptr == NULL) {
printf("Memory reallocation failed!\n");
exit(1);
}
    // Use the reallocated memory
for (int i = elements; i < newelements; i++) {
ptr[i] = i + 1;
printf("%d ", ptr[i]);
}
    // Free the allocated memory
free(ptr);
    return 0;
}
```

Output:

1 2 3 4 5 6 7 8 9 10 11 12

The above example uses malloc to allocate memory for an array of 6 integers. After using up the allocated memory, I found that I needed to store 12 elements instead. Use realloc to increase the block size of allocated memory to accommodate additional elements. It then assigns a value to the newly allocated memory and prints it. Finally, use the free function to free the allocated memory.

NOTE: Remember to always use the free function to free dynamically allocated memory after you finish using the free function to avoid memory leaks.

Exercise-16

1. Write a C program that dynamically allocates memory for an integer array of size 'x' entered by the user. Initialize the array with values from 1 to 'n' and display the array elements
2. Implement a program that dynamically allocates memory for a string entered by the user. Reverse the string using dynamic memory allocation and display the reversed string.
3. Create a program that dynamically allocates memory for a 2D array of size m x n entered by the user. Initialize the array with random numbers and display the array elements.

CHAPTER SEVENTEEN

Preprocessor Directives

Preprocessor directives in C are instructions that are processed by the preprocessor before the actual compilation of the code begins. These directives provide a way to modify the source code at the preprocessing stage. Here's an overview of the commonly used preprocessor directives in C:

1. `#include`:

The `#include` directive is used to include header files in the source code. It allows you to use functions, constants, and other declarations defined in the included files.

```
#include <stdio.h>
#include "myheadername.h"
```

2. `#define`:

The `#define` directive is used to create a macro. It assigns a name to a constant value, expression, or function-like macro.

```
#define PI 3.141
#define MAX(y, z) ((y) > (z) ? (y) : (z))
```

3. `#ifdef`, `#ifndef`, `#else`, and `#endif`:

These directives are used for conditional compilation. They allow code to be compiled based on whether a certain macro is defined (`#ifdef`), not defined (`#ifndef`), or for an alternative condition (`#else`).

```
#ifdef DEBUG
printf("Debugging mode\n");
#else
printf("Normal mode\n");
#endif
```

4. `#if`, `#elif`, and `#endif`:

These directives are used for conditional compilation based on constant expressions. They allow code to be compiled based on the evaluation of preprocessor expressions.

```
#if defined(PL_X)
// Code for platform X
#elif defined(PL_Y)
// Code for platform Y
#else
// Default code
#endif
```

5. `#pragma`:

The `#pragma` directive provides compiler-specific instructions to control various aspects of the compilation process.

```
#pragma warning(disable: 3657)
#pragma pack(1)
```

These are some of the commonly used preprocessor directives in C. They offer flexibility and allow you to control the compilation process, include necessary files, define macros, and conditionally compile sections of code.

Exercise-17

1. What is a preprocessor directive in C? Give an example.

2. How do you include a header file in your C program using a preprocessor directive? Provide an example.

3. What is the purpose of the "#define" directive in C? Explain with an example.

4. How do you use the "#ifdef" and "#ifndef" directives in C? Provide a scenario where these directives can be useful.

5. What is the purpose of the "#pragma" directive in C? Give an example of how it can be used.

6. How do you concatenate two strings using the preprocessor directives in C? Provide an example.

Exercise-1

1. Explain the difference between high-level and low-level programming languages. Give examples of each.

Answer:

a. High-level programming languages:

- High-level languages are designed to be human-readable and provide a high level of abstraction from the underlying hardware.
- They are closer to natural languages and use English-like syntax, making them easier to learn and understand for programmers.
- High-level languages offer built-in functions and libraries, allowing programmers to perform complex tasks with minimal code.
- They are generally platform-independent and provide portability, meaning the same code can be executed on different platforms with minimal modifications.

Examples of high-level programming languages include:

- Python: Known for its simplicity and readability, Python is widely used for web development, data analysis, and artificial intelligence applications.
- Java: A versatile language used for developing cross-platform applications, Java is known for its robustness and scalability.
- C#: Developed by Microsoft, C# is primarily used for Windows-based software development and is a popular language for creating desktop applications and games.

b. Low-level programming languages:

- Low-level languages are closer to machine code and provide a higher level of control over hardware resources.
- They are designed to be more efficient and have direct access to hardware, making them suitable for system-level programming and tasks that require precise control over memory and processing.
- Low-level languages often require manual memory management and have fewer built-in abstractions compared to high-level languages.

Examples of low-level programming languages include:

- Assembly language: Assembly language is specific to a particular processor architecture and uses mnemonics to represent machine instructions. It provides a direct correspondence to machine code instructions.
- C: Although C is often considered a high-level language, it is also considered a low-level language due to its close relationship with hardware and its ability to directly manipulate memory and perform low-level operations.

2. How do you install Dev C++ on your computer? Provide step-by-step instructions.

Answer:

- To install Dev C++ on your computer, you can follow these step-by-step instructions:
- Visit the official Dev-C++ website: Go to https://sourceforge.net/projects/orwelldevcpp/ in your web browser.
- Download the installation file: On the Dev-C++ project page, click on the "Download" button to download the latest version of Dev-C++. Make sure to choose the appropriate version for your operating system (Windows).
- Run the installation file: Once the download is complete, locate the downloaded file (usually in your Downloads folder) and double-click on it to run the installation.
- Start the installation process: In the installation wizard, you will see a welcome screen. Click on the "Next" button to proceed.
- Review the license agreement: Read the license agreement carefully, and if you agree, select the option to accept the terms. Then click on the "Next" button.
- Choose the installation components: Dev-C++ provides additional tools and libraries that you can choose to install. By default, the necessary components are selected. You can keep the default selection or customize it based on your requirements. Click on the "Next" button to proceed.
- Select the installation directory: Choose the folder where you want Dev-C++ to be installed or keep the default location. Click on the "Next" button to continue.
- Choose the start menu folder: Select the folder where you want the Dev-C++ shortcuts to appear in the Start menu. You can keep the default selection or specify a different folder. Click on the "Next" button.
- Select additional tasks (optional): The installer may provide additional tasks, such as creating a desktop shortcut or adding file associations. Choose the desired options or leave them unchecked. Click on the "Next" button.
- Ready to install: Review the summary of your installation preferences. If everything looks correct, click on the "Install" button to start the installation process.
- Wait for the installation to complete: The installation process may take a few moments. Once it finishes, you will see a confirmation screen.
- Launch Dev-C++: By default, the option to launch Dev-C++ after installation is selected. If it is not, you can manually open Dev-C++ from the Start menu or desktop shortcut.

3. What are the basic components of a C program? Explain each component briefly.
Answer:

- Header Files: Header files contain function prototypes and declarations necessary for the program. They are included using the #include preprocessor directive at the beginning of the program. Examples of commonly used header files are <stdio.h> for standard input/output operations and <stdlib.h> for memory allocation functions.
- Functions: Functions are the building blocks of a C program. They are self-contained blocks of code that perform specific tasks. Functions have a name, optional parameters, a return type, and a function body. They can be predefined

(from standard libraries) or user-defined. Functions are used for code modularity, reusability, and better organization.

- Variables: Variables are used to store and manipulate data in a C program. They have a data type that determines the kind of data they can hold, such as integers (int), floating-point numbers (float), characters (char), etc. Variables must be declared before they can be used and are defined by a name and a data type.
- Statements: Statements are individual instructions or actions performed in a program. They are written to carry out specific operations and can include assignments, calculations, control flow, and function calls. Statements are terminated by a semicolon (;).
- Comments: Comments are non-executable lines used for documentation and explanations within the code. They are ignored by the compiler and serve to improve code readability. Comments can be single-line (//) or multi-line (/* ... */) and are useful for providing context and clarifying code functionality.
- Control Structures: Control structures determine the flow of program execution based on conditions and decisions. They allow the program to make choices, repeat sections of code, or skip sections altogether. Common control structures in C include conditional statements (if-else, switch-case) and loops (for, while, do-while).
- Input and Output: Input and output operations are essential for interacting with the user and displaying results. C provides various functions from the <stdio.h> header file, such as scanf() for input and printf() for output. These functions allow reading input values and displaying information on the screen.

4. Why is C considered a popular programming language? List some advantages of using C.
Answer:

- C is considered a popular programming language due to several advantages it offers. Here are some key reasons why C has gained popularity:
- Efficiency: C allows for low-level manipulation of memory and direct access to hardware resources. It offers efficient code execution and enables programmers to optimize performance, making it suitable for system-level programming and applications that require high efficiency.
- Portability: C programs can be compiled and run on different platforms with minimal modifications. This portability is achieved through the availability of compilers for various operating systems and the language's adherence to standard specifications, allowing code to be easily migrated across different platforms.
- Flexibility: C provides a wide range of data types, operators, and control structures, offering flexibility in programming. It allows for precise control over memory and resources, making it suitable for developing applications where control and fine-grained manipulation are essential.
- Speed: C is known for its fast execution speed. The language provides low-level access to memory and efficient handling of system resources, allowing developers to write optimized code that executes quickly.

- Extensive Libraries: C has a vast collection of libraries, both standard libraries and third-party libraries, that provide additional functionality and pre-implemented solutions for common tasks. These libraries simplify development, allowing programmers to leverage existing code and focus on specific application logic.
- Legacy Code and Compatibility: C has been in use for several decades and has a large codebase of existing applications and libraries. This extensive codebase ensures compatibility and provides a wealth of resources for developers. Additionally, C has influenced the design of many other programming languages, making it easier for C programmers to transition to other languages and vice versa.
- Low-Level Programming Capabilities: C allows direct memory manipulation, bitwise operations, and pointer arithmetic, making it suitable for tasks that require low-level control, such as device drivers, operating systems, and embedded systems development.
- Industry Support: C has strong industry support and is widely used in various domains, including systems programming, embedded systems, game development, scientific computing, and more. Many operating systems, compilers, and development tools are built using C, further solidifying its popularity.

5. Provide a brief overview of the history of the C programming language. Who created it and when?

Answer:

The C programming language was created by Dennis Ritchie at Bell Laboratories in the early 1970s. Ritchie, along with Ken Thompson, developed C as an evolution of the earlier programming language called B, which was used to implement the UNIX operating system.

The development of C began around 1969 when Thompson wanted to write an operating system for a digital version of the PDP-7 minicomputer using an assembly language. However, he found assembly language too restrictive and wanted a higher-level language that would offer more flexibility and portability. That led to the creation of B, an interpreted programming language.

As B evolved, it became apparent that a compiled language would provide better performance and efficiency. Thus, Dennis Ritchie began developing a new programming language, originally called "New B," which later became known as C. Ritchie aimed to improve upon B by introducing features that would enhance code portability, modularity, and efficiency.

The first version of the C language was implemented on a DEC PDP-11 computer using an early version of the UNIX operating system. As the language developed, its popularity grew within the research community and industry due to its flexibility, efficiency, and portability across different hardware platforms.

In 1978, Brian Kernighan and Dennis Ritchie published "The C Programming Language," commonly known as the "K&R C" or "K&R C book." This influential book served as a comprehensive guide to the language, contributing to its widespread adoption and establishing C as a standard programming language.

C became particularly popular during the 1980s with the rise of the UNIX operating system and the development of various software tools and applications. Its simplicity, efficiency, and low-level capabilities made it suitable for systems programming, and it became the language of choice for many operating systems and compiler implementations.

Over time, C influenced the development of numerous programming languages, including C++, C#, Objective-C, and many others. Its influence is still evident today, as C remains a widely used and respected programming language, with a rich ecosystem of libraries, frameworks, and tools supporting its usage in diverse domains.

6. What are the key features of the C programming language that make it widely used in various domains?

Answer:

The key features of the C programming language that contribute to its widespread usage in various domains are as follows:

- Efficiency and Performance: C allows for low-level memory manipulation and direct hardware access, making it highly efficient. It provides control over system resources, allowing programmers to optimize code for performance-critical applications.
- Portability: C programs can be compiled and run on different platforms with minimal modifications. This portability is facilitated by the availability of C compilers for various operating systems and adherence to standardized language specifications.
- Flexibility: C offers a wide range of data types, operators, and control structures, enabling programmers to have precise control over memory and system resources. It supports both procedural and structured programming paradigms, providing flexibility in coding styles.
- Modularity and Reusability: C supports modular programming through functions and libraries. It allows programmers to break down complex problems into smaller, manageable units (functions) that can be reused and combined to build larger systems. Libraries provide pre-implemented solutions for common tasks, promoting code reuse and saving development time.
- Extensive Standard Library: C comes with a comprehensive standard library that provides functions for input/output operations, string handling, memory management, mathematical computations, and more. The standard library simplifies development by providing a set of commonly used functionalities.
- Low-Level Capabilities: C allows direct manipulation of memory, bitwise operations, and pointer arithmetic. This makes it suitable for tasks that require low-level control, such as systems programming, embedded systems, device drivers, and operating systems development.
- Industry Support and Legacy Code: C has strong industry support and a vast codebase of existing applications and libraries. It is widely used in domains such as operating systems, networking, embedded systems, game development, scientific computing, and more. Many operating systems, compilers, and development tools are implemented in C, contributing to its widespread usage and availability of resources.
- Language Interoperability: C can interface with other programming languages, enabling seamless integration with code written in different languages. This feature allows C to be used in projects that require interlanguage communication or integration with existing codebases.

7. Describe the concept of variables in C. How are variables declared and used in C programs?

Answer:

variables are used to store and manipulate data. They represent named locations in memory where values can be stored and retrieved during program execution. Variables have a specific data type, a name, and a value associated with them.

Here's an explanation of how variables are declared and used in C programs:

Declaration of Variables: To declare a variable in C, you need to specify its data type and give it a name. The syntax for variable declaration is as follows:

data_type variable_name;

For example, to declare an integer variable named age, you would write:

int age;

In this declaration, int is the data type representing integers, and age is the variable name.

Initialization of Variables: Variables can be initialized with an initial value at the time of declaration. For example:

int age = 25;

In this case, the variable age is declared and assigned an initial value of 25 at the same time.

Assignment of Values: After declaring and optionally initializing a variable, you can assign new values to it using the assignment operator (=). For example:

age = 30;

This statement assigns the value 30 to the age variable, overwriting its previous value.

Usage of Variables: Variables can be used in various ways within a C program. They can be used in calculations, assignments, conditional statements, loops, and function calls. Here are a few examples:

Calculation:

int num1 = 5;
int num2 = 10;
int sum = num1 + num2;

In this example, the variables num1 and num2 are used in the calculation of the variable sum.

Conditional Statements:

int age = 20;
if (age >= 18)
{
printf("You are an adult.\n");
}

Here, the variable age is used in the condition of the if statement to determine if the person is an adult.

Loops:

int i;
for (i = 0; i < 5; i++) {
printf("%d\n", i);
}

In this example, the variable i is used as the loop counter in a for loop.

Function Calls:

```
    int square(int num) {
return num * num;
}
    int result = square(4);
```
The variable num is used as a parameter in the square function, and the returned value is assigned to the variable result.

Variables in C can store and manipulate different types of data, such as integers, floating-point numbers, characters, and more. They play a fundamental role in storing and processing information during program execution.

8. Explain the significance of control structures in C programming. Give examples of different control structures.

Answer:

Control structures are essential components of C programming that allow the program to make decisions, control the flow of execution, and perform repetitive tasks. They determine which code blocks are executed based on specified conditions, enabling the program to respond dynamically to different situations. Control structures provide the ability to make choices, iterate over code blocks, and execute different sections of code based on specific conditions.

Here are some examples of different control structures in C:

If-else Statement:

The if-else statement allows for conditional execution of code. It evaluates a condition and executes a block of code if the condition is true, and an alternative block if the condition is false. For example:

```
    int num = 10;
if (num > 0) {
printf("The number is positive.\n");
} else {
printf("The number is non-positive.\n");
}
```

Switch Statement: The switch statement allows for multi-way branching based on the value of an expression. It evaluates the expression and executes different code blocks based on the matching case values. For example:

```
    int day = 2;
switch (day) {
case 1:
printf("Monday\n");
break;
case 2:
printf("Tuesday\n");
break;
case 3:
printf("Wednesday\n");
break;
default:
printf("Invalid day\n");
}
```

While Loop: The while loop executes a block of code repeatedly as long as a condition remains true. It evaluates the condition before each iteration. For example:

```
    int i = 0;
while (i < 5) {
printf("%d\n", i);
i++;
}
```

For Loop: The for loop provides a concise way to perform iterative tasks. It consists of three parts: initialization, condition, and increment/decrement. The loop executes the code block as long as the condition remains true. For example:

```
    for (int i = 0; i < 5; i++) {
printf("%d\n", i);
}
```

These control structures provide the means to control the flow of execution, make decisions based on conditions, and perform iterative tasks. They are fundamental tools in C programming, enabling developers to create dynamic and responsive programs.

9. What are functions in C? How are they defined and used? Provide an example of a function in C.

Answer:

Functions in C are self-contained blocks of code that perform specific tasks. They are used to modularize the code, promote code reuse, and improve program organization and readability. Functions have a name, optional parameters, a return type, and a function body.

Here's an explanation of how functions are defined and used in C:

Function Definition: A function is defined by specifying its return type, name, and parameters (if any) within a code block. The general syntax for defining a function in C is as follows:

```
    return_type function_name(parameters) {
// Function body with code to be executed
// Return statement (if the function has a return type)
}
```

- return_type: Specifies the type of value the function returns (e.g., int, float, void for no return value).
- function_name: A unique identifier for the function.
- parameters: Optional input values passed to the function for processing.

Here's an example of a function that calculates the square of a number:

```
    int square(int num) {
int result = num * num;
return result;
}
```

In this example:

- int is the return type, indicating that the function returns an integer.
- square is the name of the function.
- (int num) is the parameter list, specifying an integer parameter named num.

- The function body calculates the square of num and assigns the result to the variable result.
- The return statement returns the value of result as the output of the function.

Function Usage: To use a function in C, you need to call it by its name and provide the necessary arguments (if any). The function call can be used in expressions, assignments, or as standalone statements. Here's an example of how to use the square function defined earlier:

```
int main() {
int number = 5;
int squared = square(number);
printf("The square of %d is %d\n", number, squared);
return 0;
}
```

In this example:
The main function is the entry point of the program.
An integer variable named number is declared and assigned the value 5.
The square function is called with the number variable as an argument.
The returned value from the square function is assigned to the squared variable.
The printf function is used to display the result.
The output of this program would be: "The square of 5 is 25".

Functions allow for code modularity, reusability, and better organization. They can be used to encapsulate specific tasks, making the code more manageable and easier to understand. By dividing the program into smaller functions, it becomes easier to debug, maintain, and enhance the codebase.

10. Discuss the importance of data types in C. Provide examples of different data types and their uses.

Answer:

Data types play a crucial role in C programming as they determine the type and size of data that variables can hold. They provide a way to define the nature of data and the operations that can be performed on it. Here are the key reasons why data types are important in C:

- Memory Allocation: Data types help in allocating the appropriate amount of memory required to store data. Different data types have different memory sizes, and using the correct data type ensures efficient memory utilization.
- Data Integrity: Data types provide strict rules for the representation of data. They enforce constraints on the range of values that variables can hold, ensuring data integrity and preventing unintended data manipulation or errors.
- Operation Compatibility: Different data types support different operations. By using the appropriate data type, you ensure that operations performed on variables are compatible and yield accurate results. For example, arithmetic operations on integers differ from those on floating-point numbers.
- Code Readability: Data types convey the intended purpose of variables and make the code more readable and self-explanatory. By using descriptive data types, it becomes easier for other programmers to understand the purpose and expected behavior of variables.

Here are some commonly used data types in C:

- int: Used for storing whole numbers (integers) without decimal places. For example: int age = 25;
- float: Used for storing floating-point numbers with decimal places. For example: float temperature = 98.6;
- double: Similar to float but with higher precision and a larger range. Used for storing double-precision floating-point numbers. For example: double pi = 3.14159;
- char: Used for storing individual characters. For example: char grade = 'A';
- short: Used for storing smaller integers. Typically occupies less memory than int. For example: short count = 1000;
- long: Used for storing larger integers. Typically occupies more memory than int. For example: long population = 7896541230;
- unsigned: Used to represent non-negative values of a data type. For example: unsigned int score = 95;
- void: Used to indicate the absence of a specific data type. Often used as a return type for functions that do not return a value.

Exercise-2

1. What is the purpose of using structures in C? Provide an example of a structure declaration and explain its components.

Answer:

The purpose of using structures in C is to group related data elements of different types into a single unit, allowing for better organization, abstraction, and manipulation of complex data.Here's an example of a structure declaration and an explanation of its components:

```
struct Emp {
int empID;
  char name[50];
  int age;

};
```

In this example, we have declared a structure named "Emp" The structure contains four components or members:

1. `empID`: This member is of type `int` and represents the unique identifier for a employee.
2. `name`: This member is an array of characters (`char`) with a size of 50, representing the name of the employee.
3. `age`: This member is of type `int` and stores the age of the Employee.

By grouping these related data elements together within a structure, you can create instances of the structure that represent individual empolyees, each having their own empID, name, age. This allows for easier organization and manipulation of employees data within your C program, simplifying tasks such as sorting, searching, and accessing specific attributes of an employee.

2. Write a program to print "Hello World!".

Answer:

```
#include <stdio.h>
  int main() {
printf("Hello World!\n");
return 0;
}
```

3. Write program to add two numbers using scanf and printf in C

Answer:

```
#include <stdio.h>
  int main() {
int num1, num2, sum;
  printf("Enter the first number: ");
scanf("%d", &num1);
```

```
    printf("Enter the second number: ");
scanf("%d", &num2);
    sum = num1 + num2;
    printf("The sum of %d and %d is %d\n", num1, num2, sum);
    return 0;
}
```

4. Write a C program that declares a structure called "" with the following members: name (string), age (integer), and height (float). Initialize the structure with data and print the values of its members using printf.

Answer:

```
#include <stdio.h>
    struct Person {
char name[50];
int age;
float height;
};
    int main() {
struct Person person1; // Declare a structure variable
    // Initialize the structure members
strcpy(person1.name, "Ram");
person1.age = 22;
person1.height = 6.2;
    // Print the values of structure members
printf("Name: %s\n", person1.name);
printf("Age: %d\n", person1.age);
printf("Height: %.2f\n", person1.height);
    return 0;
}
```

Output:

```
Name: Ram
Age: 22
Height: 6.2
```

5. Discuss the importance of comments in C programs. Provide examples of single-line and multi-line comments in C.

Answer:

The importance of comments in C programs:

- Code Documentation: Comments provide essential documentation for und erstanding the purpose, functionality, and logic of code. They help fellow developers (including yourself in the future) to comprehend the code's intention and facilitate maintenance and troubleshooting.
- Code Readability: Comments enhance code readability by explaining com plex algorithms, providing context, and clarifying the reasoning behind s pecific implementation choices. Well-commented code is easier

to understand and maintain, especially for larger and collaborative projects.
- Code Debugging: Comments can be used to temporarily disable code segments for debugging purposes. By commenting out specific lines or blocks, you can isolate and identify issues without deleting code permanently. This approach allows for easy toggling and helps in tracking down bugs.
- Code Modification: Comments make it easier to modify and update code. When revisiting code after a period of time, comments serve as reminders of the code's functionality, allowing for quicker and safer modifications.

Examples of single-line and multi-line comments in C:
Single-line comments in C begin with `//` and continue until the end of the line. They are useful for brief explanations or annotations.

```c
int  age = 25;  // Initialize  the age  variable  to  25
```

Multi-line comments in C start with `/*` and end with `*/`. They are suitable for longer explanations or documenting entire sections of code.

```c
/* This  function  calculates  the sum of  two  integers
   and  returns  the  result. It  takes two  parameters,
   num1 and  num2, and  returns  their sum.  */
int  calculateSum(int  num1, int  num2) {
   return  num1 +  num2;
}
```

Using comments effectively can greatly improve code comprehension, maintainability, and collaboration among developers.

6. Write a C program to print even number in 1 to 100.
Answer:

```c
#include <stdio.h>
int main() {
int i;
   printf("Even numbers from 1 to 100:\n");
   for (i = 1; i <= 100; i++) {
if (i % 2 == 0) {
printf("%d ", i);
}
}
   printf("\n");
   return 0;
}
```

Output:

Even numbers from 1 to 100:
2 4 6 8 10 12 14 16 18 20 22 24 26 28 30 32 34 36 38 40 42 44 46 48 50 52 54 56 58 60 62 64 66 68 70 72 74 76 78 80 82 84 86 88 90 92 94 96 98 100

7.Write a Program in C to print Your name.

Answer:

```c
#include <stdio.h>
int main() {
printf("Your name\n");
return 0;
}
```

Output:

Your name

Exercise-3

1. Write a program to find the size of various data types (int, float, double, char) in C.

Answer:

```
#include <stdio.h>
int main() {
printf("Size of int: %lu bytes\n", sizeof(int));
printf("Size of float: %lu bytes\n", sizeof(float));
printf("Size of double: %lu bytes\n", sizeof(double));
printf("Size of char: %lu bytes\n", sizeof(char));

return 0;
}
```

output:

```
    Size of int: 4 bytes
Size of float: 4 bytes
Size of double: 8 bytes
Size of char: 1 byte
```

2. Write a program that accepts an integer input and displays its binary representation.

Answer:

```
#include <stdio.h>
void displayBinary(int num) {
if (num == 0) {
printf("Binary: 0\n");
return;
}
    int binary[32];
int index = 0;
    while (num > 0) {
binary[index] = num % 2;
num /= 2;
index++;
}
    printf("Binary: ");
for (int i = index - 1; i >= 0; i--) {
printf("%d", binary[i]);
}
printf("\n");
}
    int main() {
int num;
    printf("Enter an integer: ");
scanf("%d", &num);
    displayBinary(num);
    return 0;
}
```

Output:
    Enter an integer: 10
Binary: 1010

3. Write a program to swap two integers without using a temporary variable.

Answer:

```c
#include <stdio.h>
void swap(int *a, int *b) {
*a = *a + *b;
*b = *a - *b;
*a = *a - *b;
}
int main() {
int num1, num2;
    printf("Enter first number: ");
scanf("%d", &num1);
    printf("Enter second number: ");
scanf("%d", &num2);
    printf("Before swapping:\n");
printf("First number: %d\n", num1);
printf("Second number: %d\n", num2);
    swap(&num1, &num2);
    printf("After swapping:\n");
printf("First number: %d\n", num1);
printf("Second number: %d\n", num2);
    return 0;
}
```

Output :-
    Enter first number: 10
Enter second number: 20
Before swapping:
First number: 10
Second number: 20
After swapping:
First number: 20
Second number: 10

4. Write a program to convert a decimal number to its binary equivalent using bitwise operators.

Answer:

```c
#include <stdio.h>
void decimalToBinary(int num) {
if (num == 0) {
printf("Binary: 0\n");
return;
}
int binary[32];
int index = 0;
```

```c
    while (num > 0) {
binary[index] = num & 1;
num >>= 1;
index++;
}
    printf("Binary: ");
for (int i = index - 1; i >= 0; i--) {
printf("%d", binary[i]);
}
printf("\n");
}
    int main() {
int num;
    printf("Enter a decimal number: ");
scanf("%d", &num);
    decimalToBinary(num);
    return 0;
}
```

Output:
Enter a decimal number: 10
Binary: 1010

5. Write a program to find the maximum and minimum values of the data types int, float, and double.

Answer:

```c
    #include <stdio.h>
#include <limits.h>
#include <float.h>
    int main() {
printf("Maximum and Minimum Values:\n");
    printf("Int:\n");
printf("Maximum: %d\n", INT_MAX);
printf("Minimum: %d\n", INT_MIN);
    printf("Float:\n");
printf("Maximum: %f\n", FLT_MAX);
printf("Minimum: %f\n", FLT_MIN);
    printf("Double:\n");
printf("Maximum: %lf\n", DBL_MAX);
printf("Minimum: %lf\n", DBL_MIN);
    return 0;
}
```

Output:
    Maximum and Minimum Values:
Int:
Maximum: 2147483647
Minimum: -2147483648
Float:

Maximum: 340282346638528859811704183484516925440.000000

Minimum: 0.000000

Double:

Maximum:

17976931348623157081452742373170435679807056752584499659891747680315726078
00285387605895586327668781715404589535143824642343213268894641827684675467
03537516986049910576551282076245490090389328944075868508455133942304583236
90322294816580855933212334827479782620414472316873817718091929988125040402
6184124858368

Minimum: 2.225074e-308

6. Write a program to check if a given number is a power of 2 using bitwise operators.

Answer:

```
#include <stdio.h>
int isPowerOfTwo(int num) {
if (num <= 0)
return 0;

return ((num & (num - 1)) == 0);
}
int main() {
int num;
    printf("Enter a number: ");
scanf("%d", &num);
    if (isPowerOfTwo(num))
printf("%d is a power of 2.\n");
else
printf("%d is not a power of 2.\n");
    return 0;
}
```

Output:

Enter a number: 8

8 is a power of 2.

Enter a number: 10

10 is not a power of 2.

7. Write a program to reverse a given integer number and check if it is a palindrome.

Answer:

```
#include <stdio.h>
int reverseNumber(int num) {
int reversedNum = 0;
    while (num != 0) {
int remainder = num % 10;
reversedNum = reversedNum * 10 + remainder;
num /= 10;
}
    return reversedNum;
}
```

```c
    int isPalindrome(int num) {
int reversedNum = reverseNumber(num);
    if (num == reversedNum)
return 1;
else
return 0;
}
    int main() {
int num;
    printf("Enter an integer: ");
scanf("%d", &num);
    if (isPalindrome(num))
printf("%d is a palindrome.\n");
else
printf("%d is not a palindrome.\n");
    return 0;
}
```

Output:
    Enter an integer: 12321
12321 is a palindrome.
    Enter an integer: 12345
12345 is not a palindrome.

8. Write a program to convert a given character to its corresponding ASCII value.
    Answer:
```c
    #include <stdio.h>
    int main() {
char character;
    printf("Enter a character: ");
scanf("%c", &character);
    printf("ASCII value of '%c' is %d\n", character, character);
    return 0;
}
```

Output:
    Enter a character: A
ASCII value of 'A' is 65

9. Write a program to find the factorial of a given number using recursion.
    Answer:
```c
    #include <stdio.h>
    unsigned long long factorial(unsigned int num) {
if (num == 0)
return 1;
else
return num * factorial(num - 1);
}
```

```c
    int main() {
unsigned int num;
    printf("Enter a positive integer: ");
scanf("%u", &num);
    unsigned long long result = factorial(num);
    printf("Factorial of %u is %llu\n", num, result);
    return 0;
}
```

Output:
    Enter a positive integer: 5
Factorial of 5 is 120

10. Write a program to calculate the sum of digits in a given integer number.

Answer:
```c
#include <stdio.h>
int sumOfDigits(int num) {
int sum = 0;
    while (num != 0) {
int digit = num % 10;
sum += digit;
num /= 10;
}
    return sum;
}
    int main() {
int num;
    printf("Enter an integer: ");
scanf("%d", &num);
    int result = sumOfDigits(num);
    printf("Sum of digits in %d is %d\n", num, result);
    return 0;
}
```

Output:
    Enter an integer: 12345
Sum of digits in 12345 is 15

Exercise-4

1. Declare a variable of type `int` named `age` and assign it the value 25. Print the value of `age` to the console.

Answer:

Program:

```
#include <stdio.h>
    int main() {
int age = 20;
printf("Age: %d\n", age);
return 0;
}
```

In this program, we declare an `int` variable named `age` and assign it the value 20 using the assignment operator `=`.

Then, we use the `printf` function to print the value of `age` to the console. The `%d` placeholder is used to represent the integer value, and it is replaced with the value of `age` when printed.

When you run the program, it will output:

Age: 20

This confirms that the variable `age` is declared and assigned the value 20, and it is successfully printed to the console.

Output:

Age: 20

2. Create two variables, `length` and `width`, both of type `float`. Assign the values 5.7 and 3.2 respectively. Calculate the area of a rectangle using these variables and print the result.

Answer:

```
#include <stdio.h>
    int main() {
float length = 7.5;
float width = 2.2;
    float area = length * width;
    printf("Length: %.2f\n", length);
printf("Width: %.2f\n", width);
printf("Area: %.2f\n", area);
    return 0;
```

Output:

Length: 7.50

Width: 2.20

Area: 16.50

3. Declare a variable `character` of type `char` and assign it the value 'A'. Print the character to the console.

Answer:

```
#include <stdio.h>
```

```
   int main() {
char character = 'I';
printf("Character: %c\n", character);
return 0;
}
```

Output:
   Character: I
   4. Declare a variable `isStudent` of type `int` and assign it a value of either 0 or 1 to represent whether a person is a student or not. Print "You are a student" if `isStudent` is 1, and "You are not a student" if `isStudent` is 0.
   Answer:
```
   #include <stdio.h>
   int main() {
int isStudent = 1;
   if (isStudent == 1) {
printf("You are a student\n");
} else {
printf("You are not a student\n");
}
   return 0;
}
```

Output:
   When you run the program with **isStudent assigned a value of 1**, it will output:
   You are a student
   If you change the value of **isStudent to 0**, it will output:
   You are not a student
   5. Declare two variables, `num1` and `num2`, both of type `int`. Take input from the user for these two variables using `scanf`, calculate their sum, and print the result.
   Answer:
```
   #include <stdio.h>
   int main() {
int num1, num2, sum;
   printf("Enter the first number: ");
scanf("%d", &num1);
   printf("Enter the second number: ");
scanf("%d", &num2);
   sum = num1 + num2;
   printf("The sum of %d and %d is %d\n", num1, num2, sum);
   return 0;
}
```
   Output:
   The sum of 22 and 5 is 27
   6. Create a variable `pi` of type `float` and assign it the value 3.14159. Declare another variable `radius` of type `float` and assign it any value of your choice. Calculate the area of a circle using the formula `area = pi * radius * radius` and print the result.

Answer:
```c
#include <stdio.h>
int main() {
float pi = 3.14159;
float radius = 3.2;
    float area = pi * radius * radius;
    printf("Radius: %.2f\n", radius);
printf("Area: %.2f\n", area);
    return 0;
}
```
Output:
Radius: 3.20
Area: 32.15

7. Declare a variable `name` of type `char` array with a size of 20. Take input from the user for the name using `scanf` and print a personalized greeting like "Hello, [Name]!".
Answer:
```c
#include <stdio.h>
int main() {
char name[20];
    printf("Enter your name: ");
scanf("%s", name);
    printf("Hello, %s!\n", name);
    return 0;
}
```
Output:
Hello, Name!

8. Create a variable `count` of type `int` and initialize it with 0. Use a loop to increment the value of `count` by 1, and print its value at each iteration until it reaches 10.
Answer:
```c
#include <stdio.h>
int main() {
int count = 0;
    while (count <= 10) {
printf("Count: %d\n", count);
count++;
}
    return 0;
}
```
Output:
Count: 0
Count: 1
Count: 2
Count: 3
Count: 4
Count: 5

```
Count: 6
Count: 7
Count: 8
Count: 9
Count: 10
```

Exercise-5

1. what is Constant in C?

Answer:

In C, a constant is a fixed value that cannot be modified during program execution. It is a value that remains unchanged throughout the program's execution. Constants are used to represent fixed or unchanging values, such as numbers, characters, or strings.

Constants in C can be of different types, such as integer constants, floating-point constants, character constants, and string constants.

In short, a constant in C is a value that cannot be altered once it is assigned, providing a way to represent fixed values in the program.

2. what is the differnece between scope and the variable ?

Answer:

- Scope refers to the visibility or accessibility of a variable within a program. It defines where a variable can be accessed or referenced. It determines the portion of the program where the variable is valid and can be used.
- A variable, on the other hand, is a named storage location in the computer's memory used to store data. It represents a value that can be assigned, read, and modified during program execution. Variables are used to hold and manipulate data within a program.

3. write an example for 3 numberic constant in c.

Answer:

```c
#include <stdio.h>
int main() {
const int NUMBER1 = 10; // Integer constant
const float NUMBER2 = 3.14; // Floating-point constant
const double NUMBER3 = 2.71828; // Double constant

printf("Numeric Constants:\n");
printf("Number 1: %d\n", NUMBER1);
printf("Number 2: %f\n", NUMBER2);
printf("Number 3: %lf\n", NUMBER3);

return 0;
}
```

In this program, we declare three numeric constants of different types:

NUMBER1 is an integer constant with a value of 10.

NUMBER2 is a floating-point constant with a value of 3.14.

NUMBER3 is a double constant with a value of 2.71828.

The const keyword is used to declare these constants, indicating that their values cannot be modified during program execution.

In the main() function, we use printf() to display the values of these constants. The format specifiers %d, %f, and %lf are used to format and display the integer, float, and double values, respectively.

When you run this program, it will display the values of the three numeric constants:

Numeric Constants:
Number 1: 10
Number 2: 3.140000
Number 3: 2.718280

4. what is literals?

Answer:

literals are fixed values that are directly written in the code of a program. They represent constant values of different types, such as integers, floating-point numbers, characters, and strings.

Literals are used to provide specific values to variables or to perform operations directly with these values. They are called literals because they are written literally in the program code without any computation or evaluation.

Here are a few examples of literals in C:

Integer literal: 25

Floating-point literal: 3.14

Character literal: 'A'

String literal: "Hello"

In these examples, the values 25, 3.14, 'A', and "Hello" are literals.

Literals are constant values and cannot be modified during program execution. They are directly interpreted by the compiler as specific values of their respective types.

5. How are constants stored in memory in C? Explain the memory allocation for different types of constants.

Answer:

- Integer Constants: Integer constants are typically stored as immediate values in the instruction or data segment of the program. For small integers, they can be stored directly within the instruction or as part of the program's data segment.
- Floating-Point Constants: Floating-point constants are typically stored as immediate values or in a dedicated floating-point constant table within the program's data segment.
- Character Constants: Character constants are usually stored as immediate values or ASCII codes within the program's instruction or data segment.
- String Constants: String constants, also known as string literals, are stored as continuous sequences of characters in the program's data segment. They are typically stored as read-only memory to ensure their immutability.

6. How constant and literals impact in C?

Answer:

- Constants: Constants are named values that remain fixed throughout the execution of a program. They allow programmers to assign meaningful names to values that should not be changed. Constants enhance code readability, improve maintainability, and provide a way to represent fixed values in a program. They can be used for various purposes such as defining mathematical or physical constants, setting configuration values, or representing fixed values in algorithms.
- Literals: Literals are fixed values that are directly written in the code. They provide specific values for variables or are used directly in operations. Literals are used to

represent constant values of different types, such as integers, floating-point numbers, characters, and strings. They allow programmers to provide immediate values without the need for additional computations or evaluations. Literals can be used for initializing variables, performing arithmetic operations, or defining constant values within the program logic.

Together, constants and literals provide a way to represent fixed values in C programs, enhancing code readability and maintainability. They help in expressing intentions clearly and accurately, making the code more self-explanatory and less prone to errors. Additionally, constants and literals contribute to the efficiency of the program by eliminating the need for repetitive calculations or computations.

Exercise-6

1. What is Operator in C?

Answer:

In C, an operator is a symbol or sequence of symbols that represents an operation to be performed on one or more operands. Operators allow you to manipulate data and perform various computations within a program. Here are the key points regarding operators in C:

1. Types of Operators:

- -Arithmetic Operators: Perform mathematical operations such as addition, subtraction, multiplication, division, and modulus.
- Relational Operators: Compare values and determine the relationship between them, returning a Boolean result (true or false).
- Logical Operators: Combine or negate Boolean expressions, allowing you to perform logical operations like AND, OR, and NOT.
- Assignment Operators: Assign a value to a variable.
- Increment/Decrement Operators: Increment or decrement the value of a variable by 1.
- Bitwise Operators: Perform operations on individual bits of operands.
- Conditional (Ternary) Operator: Provide a shorthand for if-else statements.
- Comma Operator: Evaluate multiple expressions and return the value of the last expression.

2. Precedence and Associativity: Operators have precedence and associativity, which determine the order of evaluation when multiple operators are present in an expression. Parentheses can be used to override the default precedence and specify the desired evaluation order.

3. Unary, Binary, and Ternary Operators: Operators can be unary (act on a single operand), binary (act on two operands), or ternary (act on three operands).

4. Operator Overloading: C does not support operator overloading, which means the behavior of operators cannot be modified for user-defined data types.

5. Examples:

- Arithmetic Operators: `+`, `-`, `*`, `/`, `%`
- Relational Operators: `>`, `<`, `>=`, `<=`, `==`, `!=`
- Logical Operators: `&&`, `||`, `!`
- Assignment Operators: `=`, `+=`, `-=`, `*=`, `/=`, `%=`
- Increment/Decrement Operators: `++`, `--`
- Bitwise Operators: `&`, `|`, `^`, `~`, `<<`, `>>`
- Conditional Operator: `condition ? expression1 : expression2`
- Comma Operator: `expr1, expr2`

Understanding operators is crucial for performing computations, making decisions, and manipulating data within C programs. By leveraging operators effectively, you can create powerful and efficient code.

2. Write a C program to calculate the product of two integers using the multiplication operator (*).

Answer:

```c
#include <stdio.h>
int main() {
int num1, num2, product;
    printf("Enter the first number: ");
scanf("%d", &num1);
    printf("Enter the second number: ");
scanf("%d", &num2);
    product = num1 * num2;
    printf("The product of %d and %d is %d\n", num1, num2, product);
    return 0;
}
```

Output:

The product of 5 and 8 is 40

3. Write a C program to increment an integer variable by 1 using the increment operator (++).

Answer:

```c
#include <stdio.h>
int main() {
int num = 3;
    printf("Before increment: %d\n", num);
    num++; // Increment the value of num by 1
    printf("After increment: %d\n", num);
    return 0;
}
```

Output:

Before increment: 3
After increment: 2

4. Write a C program to check if two integers are not equal using the inequality operator (!=).

Answer:

```c
#include <stdio.h>
int main() {
int num1, num2;
    printf("Enter the first number: ");
scanf("%d", &num1);
    printf("Enter the second number: ");
scanf("%d", &num2);
    if (num1 != num2) {
printf("The two numbers are not equal\n");
} else {
printf("The two numbers are equal\n");
}
    return 0;
}
```

Output:

Enter the first number:4

Enter the second number: 6
The two numbers are not equal

5. Write a C program to check if one integer is less than or equal to another using the less than or equal to operator (<=).

Answer:

```c
#include <stdio.h>
int main() {
int num1, num2;
    printf("Enter the first number: ");
scanf("%d", &num1);
    printf("Enter the second number: ");
scanf("%d", &num2);
    if (num1 <= num2) {
printf("The first number is less than or equal to the second number\n");
} else {
printf("The first number is greater than the second number\n");
}
    return 0;
}
```

Output:

Enter the first number:5
Enter the second number:8
The first number is less than or equal to the second number

6. Write a C program to perform a bitwise XOR operation on two integers using the bitwise XOR operator (^).

Answer:

```c
#include <stdio.h>
int main() {
int num1, num2, result;
    printf("Enter the first number: ");
scanf("%d", &num1);
    printf("Enter the second number: ");
scanf("%d", &num2);
    result = num1 ^ num2;
    printf("Bitwise XOR : %d\n", result);
    return 0;
}
```

Output:

Bitwise XOR : 6

7. Write a C program to swap the values of two integers without using a temporary variable, using the assignment (=) and arithmetic (+, -) operators.

Answer:

```c
#include <stdio.h>
int main() {
int num1, num2;
```

```c
    printf("Enter the first number: ");
scanf("%d", &num1);
    printf("Enter the second number: ");
scanf("%d", &num2);
    printf("Before swapping:\n");
printf("First number: %d\n", num1);
printf("Second number: %d\n", num2);
    num1 = num1 + num2;
num2 = num1 - num2;
num1 = num1 - num2;
    printf("After swapping:\n");
printf("First number: %d\n", num1);
printf("Second number: %d\n", num2);
    return 0;
}
```

Output:
```
    Before swapping:
First number: 3
Second number: 9
After swapping:
First number: 9
Second number: 3
```

8. Write a C program to perform a bitwise NOT operation on an integer using the bitwise NOT operator (~).

Answer:
```c
#include <stdio.h>
int main() {
int num;
    printf("Enter an integer: ");
scanf("%d", &num);
    int result = ~num;
    printf("Bitwise NOT result: %d\n", result);
    return 0;
}
```

Output:
```
    Bitwise NOT result: -11
```

Exercise-7

1. Write a program that accepts an integer input from the user and checks if it is positive, negative, or zero.

Answer:

```
#include <stdio.h>
int main() {
int num;
printf("Enter an integer: ");
scanf("%d", &num);
if (num > 0)
printf("%d is positive.\n", num);
else if (num < 0)
printf("%d is negative.\n", num);
else
printf("The number is zero.\n");
return 0;
}
```

output:

Enter an integer: 10

10 is positive.

Enter an integer: -5

-5 is negative.

Enter an integer: 0

The number is zero.

2. Write a program that accepts three numbers from the user and prints the largest number using the if-else statement.

Answer:

```
#include <stdio.h>
int main() {
int num1, num2, num3;
printf("Enter three numbers: ");
scanf("%d %d %d", &num1, &num2, &num3);
if (num1 >= num2 && num1 >= num3)
printf("%d is the largest number.\n", num1);
else if (num2 >= num1 && num2 >= num3)
printf("%d is the largest number.\n", num2);
else
printf("%d is the largest number.\n", num3);
return 0;
}
```

Output:

Enter three numbers: 10 5 8

10 is the largest number.

Enter three numbers: 6 9 3

9 is the largest number.

Enter three numbers: 2 2 2

2 is the largest number.

3. Write a program that prints all the prime numbers between 1 and 100 using a for loop and if statement.

Answer:

```
#include <stdio.h>
int main() {
int i, j;
int isPrime;
    printf("Prime numbers between 1 and 100 are:\n");
    for (i = 2; i <= 100; i++) {
isPrime = 1;
    for (j = 2; j <= i/2; j++) {
if (i % j == 0) {
isPrime = 0;
break;
}
}
    if (isPrime == 1)
printf("%d ", i);
}
    printf("\n");
    return 0;
}
```

Output

Prime numbers between 1 and 100 are:

2 3 5 7 11 13 17 19 23 29 31 37 41 43 47 53 59 61 67 71 73 79 83 89 97

4. Write a program that calculates the factorial of a given number using a while loop.

Answer:

```
#include <stdio.h>
unsigned long long factorial(unsigned int num) {
unsigned long long result = 1;
    while (num > 1) {
result *= num;
num--;
}
    return result;
}
    int main() {
unsigned int num;
    printf("Enter a positive integer: ");
scanf("%u", &num);
    unsigned long long result = factorial(num);
    printf("Factorial of %u is %llu\n", num, result);
    return 0;
}
```

Output:

Enter a positive integer: 5
Factorial of 5 is 120

5. Write a program that accepts a character from the user and checks if it is a vowel or a consonant using the switch statement.

Answer:

```c
#include <stdio.h>
int main() {
char character;
    printf("Enter a character: ");
scanf(" %c", &character);
    switch (character) {
case 'a':
case 'e':
case 'i':
case 'o':
case 'u':
case 'A':
case 'E':
case 'I':
case 'O':
case 'U':
printf("%c is a vowel.\n", character);
break;
default:
printf("%c is a consonant.\n", character);
break;
}
    return 0;
}
```

Output:
Enter a character: A
A is a vowel.
Enter a character: d
d is a consonant.

6. Write a program to find the sum of all even numbers between 1 and 50 using the do-while loop.

Answer:

```c
#include <stdio.h>
int main() {
int num = 2; // Start with the first even number
int sum = 0;
    do {
sum += num;
num += 2; // Increment by 2 to get the next even number
} while (num <= 50);
    printf("Sum of even numbers between 1 and 50: %d\n", sum);
```

```
    return 0;
}
```

Output:
  Sum of even numbers between 1 and 50: 650

7. Write a program that prints the multiplication table of a given number using a for loop.

Answer:
```
#include <stdio.h>
int main() {
int number;
    printf("Enter a number: ");
scanf("%d", &number);
    printf("Multiplication Table of %d:\n", number);
    for (int i = 1; i <= 10; i++) {
int product = number * i;
printf("%d x %d = %d\n", number, i, product);
}
    return 0;
}
```

Output:
  Enter a number: 5
Multiplication Table of 5:
5 x 1 = 5
5 x 2 = 10
5 x 3 = 15
5 x 4 = 20
5 x 5 = 25
5 x 6 = 30
5 x 7 = 35
5 x 8 = 40
5 x 9 = 45
5 x 10 = 50

8. Write a program that accepts a positive integer from the user and checks if it is a perfect number.

Answer:
```
#include <stdio.h>
int main() {
int num, sum = 0;
    printf("Enter a positive integer: ");
scanf("%d", &num);
    // Find the sum of proper divisors
for (int i = 1; i <= num / 2; i++) {
if (num % i == 0) {
sum += i;
```

```
}
}
    // Check if the number is perfect
if (sum == num) {
printf("%d is a perfect number.\n", num);
} else {
printf("%d is not a perfect number.\n", num);
}
    return 0;
}
```

Output:
    Enter a positive integer: 28
28 is a perfect number.
    Enter a positive integer: 12
12 is not a perfect number.

9. Write a program that prompts the user to enter a password and allows access only if the correct password is entered (use the if-else statement).

Answer:
```
    #include <stdio.h>
#include <string.h>
    int main() {
char password[20];
    printf("Enter the password: ");
scanf("%s", password);
    // Compare entered password with the correct password
if (strcmp(password, "password123") == 0) {
printf("Access granted. Welcome!\n");
} else {
printf("Access denied. Incorrect password.\n");
}
    return 0;
}
```

Output:
    Enter the password: password123
Access granted. Welcome!
    Enter the password: pass123
Access denied. Incorrect password.

10. Write a program that prints the Fibonacci series up to a given number using the while loop.

Answer:
```
    #include <stdio.h>
    int main() {
int limit, num1 = 0, num2 = 1, nextTerm;
    printf("Enter the limit: ");
scanf("%d", &limit);
```

```c
    printf("Fibonacci Series up to %d: %d, %d, ", limit, num1, num2);
    nextTerm = num1 + num2;
    while (nextTerm <= limit) {
printf("%d, ", nextTerm);
num1 = num2;
num2 = nextTerm;
nextTerm = num1 + num2;
}
    printf("\n");
    return 0;
}
```

Output:
    Enter the limit: 100
Fibonacci Series up to 100: 0, 1, 1, 2, 3, 5, 8, 13, 21, 34, 55, 89,

Exercise-8

1. What is array in C?

Answer:

In C, an array is a collection of elements of the same data type that are stored in contiguous memory locations. Here are the key points regarding arrays in C:

1. An array is defined as a fixed-size container that can hold a sequence of elements of the same data type. The size of an array is determined at the time of declaration.

2. Each element in an array is accessed using an index, starting from 0 for the first element and incrementing by 1 for each subsequent element.

3. An array is declared by specifying the data type of its elements, followed by the name of the array and the number of elements it can hold. For example, `int numbers[5];` declares an integer array named `numbers` that can hold 5 elements.

4. Arrays can be initialized at the time of declaration. For example, `int numbers[5] = {1, 2, 3, 4, 5};` initializes the `numbers` array with the provided values.

5. Elements in an array can be accessed using the array name followed by the index in square brackets. For example, `numbers[2]` accesses the third element in the `numbers` array.

6. The size of an array, once declared, is fixed and cannot be changed during the execution of the program.

7. In C, arrays use zero-based indexing, which means the first element is accessed using index 0, the second element with index 1, and so on.

8. Arrays are used to store and manipulate collections of data efficiently. They are often used for tasks such as storing a list of numbers, characters, strings, or any other data type.

9. C also supports multidimensional arrays, which are arrays of arrays. They allow you to store data in multiple dimensions, such as rows and columns in a matrix.

10. You can access individual elements or perform operations on the entire array using loops such as `for` or `while`.

Understanding arrays in C is essential for working with collections of data and performing various operations efficiently. They provide a structured way to store and manipulate multiple elements of the same data type.

2. List and explain the Types of Array in C.

Answer:

In C, arrays can be categorized into two main types: single-dimensional arrays and multi-dimensional arrays.

1. Single-Dimensional Arrays:

- Single-dimensional arrays, also known as one-dimensional arrays, are the simplest type of array in C. They consist of a linear collection of elements of the same data type, accessed using a single index.

- Single-dimensional arrays are declared using square brackets `[]` after the array name, indicating the size of the array. For example, `int numbers[5];` declares an integer array named `numbers` with a size of 5.

- Elements in a single-dimensional array are accessed using their index, starting from 0. For example, `numbers[2]` accesses the third element in the `numbers` array.
- Single-dimensional arrays are often used to store and manipulate sequences of data, such as lists of numbers or characters.

2. Multi-Dimensional Arrays:

- Multi-dimensional arrays extend the concept of arrays to two or more dimensions. They are essentially arrays of arrays.
- Common types of multi-dimensional arrays include two-dimensional arrays (matrices) and three-dimensional arrays (cubes or volumes).
- Multi-dimensional arrays are declared using multiple sets of square brackets `[][]`, where each set represents a dimension. For example, `int matrix[3][3];` declares a two-dimensional integer array named `matrix` with dimensions 3x3.
- Elements in a multi-dimensional array are accessed using multiple indices, representing each dimension. For example, `matrix[1][2]` a ccesses the element at the second row and third column of the `matrix` array.
- Multi-dimensional arrays are useful for representing tabular data, matrices, and other complex structures that require more than one dimension.

Both single-dimensional and multi-dimensional arrays in C offer a way to store and manipulate collections of data efficiently. The choice between them depends on the specific requirements of your program and the structure of the data you need to represent.

3. Write a C program to find the sum of all elements in an integer array.
Answer:
```
#include <stdio.h>
#define SIZE 5 // Size of the array
int main() {
  int array[SIZE] = {2, 4, 6, 8, 10};
  int sum = 0;
// Calculate the sum of array elements
  for (int i = 0; i < SIZE; i++) {
  sum += array[i];
  }
printf("Sum of array elements: %d\n", sum);
return 0;
  }
```
Output:
Sum of array elements: 30

4. Write a C program to find the maximum element in an array.
Answer:
```
#include <stdio.h>
#define SIZE 5 // Size of the array
```

```c
int main() {
  int array[SIZE] = {10, 5, 8, 12, 3};
  int max = array[0];
// Find the maximum element in the array
  for (int i = 1; i < SIZE; i++) {
  if (array[i] > max) {
  max = array[i];
  }
  }
printf("Maximum element: %d\n", max);
return 0;
  }
```
Output:
Maximum element: 12

5. Write a C program to find the minimum element in an array.
Answer:
```c
#include <stdio.h>
#define SIZE 5 // Size of the array
int main() {
  int array[SIZE] = {10, 5, 8, 12, 3};
  int min = array[0];
// Find the minimum element in the array
  for (int i = 1; i < SIZE; i++) {
  if (array[i] < min) {
  min = array[i];
  }
  }
printf("Minimum element: %d\n", min);
return 0;
  }
```
Output:
Minimum element: 3

6. Write a C program to calculate the average of elements in an array.
Answer:
```c
#include <stdio.h>
#define SIZE 5 // Size of the array
int main() {
  int array[SIZE] = {10, 5, 8, 12, 3};
  int sum = 0;
  float average;
// Calculate the sum of array elements
  for (int i = 0; i < SIZE; i++) {
  sum += array[i];
  }
// Calculate the average
  average = (float)sum / SIZE;
```

```c
printf("Average of array elements: %.2f\n", average);
return 0;
}
```
Output:
Average of array elements: 7.60

7. Write a C program to count the number of even and odd elements in an integer array.
Answer:
```c
#include <stdio.h>
#define SIZE 7 // Size of the array
int main() {
  int array[SIZE] = {12, 5, 8, 9, 10, 7, 6};
  int evenCount = 0, oddCount = 0;
// Count the number of even and odd elements
  for (int i = 0; i < SIZE; i++) {
  if (array[i] % 2 == 0) {
  evenCount++;
  } else {
  oddCount++;
  }
  }
printf("Number of even elements: %d\n", evenCount);
  printf("Number of odd elements: %d\n", oddCount);
return 0;
  }
```
Output:
Number of even elements: 4
  Number of odd elements: 3

8. Write a C program to reverse the elements in an array.
Answer:
```c
#include <stdio.h>
#define SIZE 5 // Size of the array
int main() {
  int array[SIZE] = {1, 2, 3, 4, 5};
  printf("Original array: ");
  for (int i = 0; i < SIZE; i++) {
  printf("%d ", array[i]);
  }
// Reverse the array
  int start = 0;
  int end = SIZE - 1;
  int temp;
while (start < end) {
  // Swap elements at start and end positions
  temp = array[start];
  array[start] = array[end];
  array[end] = temp;
```

```c
// Move start towards the center and end towards the center
  start++;
  end--;
  }
printf("\nReversed array: ");
  for (int i = 0; i < SIZE; i++) {
  printf("%d ", array[i]);
  }
return 0;
  }
```

Output:
Original array: 1 2 3 4 5
  Reversed array: 5 4 3 2 1

9. Write a C program to remove duplicate elements from an array.
Answer:
```c
#include <stdio.h>
#define SIZE 10 // Size of the array
int main() {
  int array[SIZE] = {1, 2, 3, 2, 4, 5, 3, 6, 7, 7};
  int uniqueArray[SIZE];
  int uniqueCount = 0;
// Remove duplicate elements from the array
  for (int i = 0; i < SIZE; i++) {
  int isDuplicate = 0;
for (int j = 0; j < uniqueCount; j++) {
  if (array[i] == uniqueArray[j]) {
  isDuplicate = 1;
  break;
  }
  }
if (!isDuplicate) {
  uniqueArray[uniqueCount] = array[i];
  uniqueCount++;
  }
  }
printf("Original array: ");
  for (int i = 0; i < SIZE; i++) {
  printf("%d ", array[i]);
  }
printf("\nArray with duplicate elements removed: ");
  for (int i = 0; i < uniqueCount; i++) {
  printf("%d ", uniqueArray[i]);
  }
return 0;
  }
```
Output:

Original array: 1 2 3 2 4 5 3 6 7 7
  Array with duplicate elements removed: 1 2 3 4 5 6 7

10. Write a C program to find the second largest element in an array.
Answer:
```c
#include <stdio.h>
#define SIZE 8 // Size of the array
int main() {
  int array[SIZE] = {10, 5, 8, 12, 3, 15, 7,0};
  int largest = array[0];
  int secondLargest = array[0];
// Find the largest element in the array
  for (int i = 1; i < SIZE; i++) {
  if (array[i] > largest) {
  secondLargest = largest;
  largest = array[i];
  } else if (array[i] > secondLargest && array[i] != largest) {
  secondLargest = array[i];
  }
  }
printf("Second largest element: %d\n", secondLargest);
return 0;
  }
```
Output:
Second largest element: 12

Exercise-9

1. Write a program to find the maximum between two numbers using a function.

Answer:

```
#include <stdio.h>
int findMaximum(int num1, int num2) {
 if (num1 > num2)
 return num1;
 else
 return num2;
 }
int main() {
 int number1, number2;
printf("Enter the first number: ");
 scanf("%d", &number1);
printf("Enter the second number: ");
 scanf("%d", &number2);
int maximum = findMaximum(number1, number2);
printf("The maximum number is: %d\n", maximum);
return 0;
 }
```

 Output:

Enter the first number: 5

 Enter the second number: 9

 The maximum number is: 9

2. Write a program to check if a given number is prime or not using a function.

Answer:

```
#include <stdio.h>
int isPrime(int number) {
 if (number <= 1)
 return 0;
for (int i = 2; i <= number / 2; i++) {
 if (number % i == 0) {
 return 0;
 }
 }
return 1;
 }
int main() {
 int num;
printf("Enter a positive integer: ");
 scanf("%d", &num);
if (isPrime(num)) {
 printf("%d is a prime number.\n", num);
 } else {
```

```
  printf("%d is not a prime number.\n", num);
  }
 return 0;
  }
```

Output:
Enter a positive integer: 17
  17 is a prime number.
Enter a positive integer: 10
  10 is not a prime number.

3. Write a program to calculate the factorial of a given number using a recursive function.

Answer:
```
#include <stdio.h>
unsigned long long factorial(unsigned int num) {
  if (num == 0)
   return 1;
   else
   return num * factorial(num - 1);
  }
int main() {
  unsigned int num;
 printf("Enter a positive integer: ");
  scanf("%u", &num);
 unsigned long long result = factorial(num);
 printf("Factorial of %u is %llu\n", num, result);
 return 0;
  }
```

Output:
Enter a positive integer: 5
  Factorial of 5 is 120

4. Write a program to swap the values of two variables using a function.

Answer:
```
#include <stdio.h>
void swap(int *a, int *b) {
  int temp = *a;
  *a = *b;
  *b = temp;
  }
int main() {
  int num1, num2;
 printf("Enter the first number: ");
  scanf("%d", &num1);
 printf("Enter the second number: ");
  scanf("%d", &num2);
 printf("Before swapping: num1 = %d, num2 = %d\n", num1, num2);
 swap(&num1, &num2);
```

```c
printf("After swapping: num1 = %d, num2 = %d\n", num1, num2);
return 0;
}
```

Output:
Enter the first number: 10
Enter the second number: 20
Before swapping: num1 = 10, num2 = 20
After swapping: num1 = 20, num2 = 10

5. Write a program to find the sum of all elements in an array using a function.

Answer:

```c
#include <stdio.h>
int findSum(int arr[], int size) {
  int sum = 0;

  for (int i = 0; i < size; i++) {
  sum += arr[i];
  }

  return sum;
  }
int main() {
  int size;

  printf("Enter the size of the array: ");
  scanf("%d", &size);

  int arr[size];

  printf("Enter the elements of the array:\n");

  for (int i = 0; i < size; i++) {
  scanf("%d", &arr[i]);
  }

  int sum = findSum(arr, size);

  printf("The sum of all elements in the array is: %d\n", sum);

  return 0;
  }
```

Output:
Enter the size of the array: 5
Enter the elements of the array:
1
2

3
4
5
The sum of all elements in the array is: 15

6. Write a program to reverse a string using a function.

Answer:

```c
#include <stdio.h>
 #include <string.h>
void reverseString(char str[]) {
  int start = 0;
  int end = strlen(str) - 1;
while (start < end) {
  char temp = str[start];
  str[start] = str[end];
  str[end] = temp;
  start++;
  end--;
  }
 }
int main() {
  char str[100];
printf("Enter a string: ");
  fgets(str, sizeof(str), stdin);
// Remove newline character from fgets
  str[strcspn(str, "\n")] = '\0';
printf("Before reversing: %s\n", str);
reverseString(str);
printf("After reversing: %s\n", str);
return 0;
 }
```

Output:
Enter a string: Hello, World!
  Before reversing: Hello, World!
  After reversing: !dlroW ,olleH

7. Write a program to calculate the area of a circle using a function.

Answer:

```c
#include <stdio.h>
#define PI 3.14159
double calculateArea(double radius) {
  return PI * radius * radius;
 }
int main() {
  double radius;
printf("Enter the radius of the circle: ");
  scanf("%lf", &radius);
double area = calculateArea(radius);
```

```c
printf("The area of the circle is: %.2lf\n", area);
return 0;
}
```

Output:
Enter the radius of the circle: 5.5
 The area of the circle is: 95.03

8. Write a program to find the LCM (Least Common Multiple) of two numbers using a function.

Answer:

```c
#include <stdio.h>
int findGCD(int num1, int num2) {
  while (num2 != 0) {
  int remainder = num1 % num2;
  num1 = num2;
  num2 = remainder;
  }
  return num1;
  }
int findLCM(int num1, int num2) {
  int gcd = findGCD(num1, num2);
  int lcm = (num1 * num2) / gcd;
  return lcm;
  }
int main() {
  int number1, number2;
printf("Enter the first number: ");
  scanf("%d", &number1);
printf("Enter the second number: ");
  scanf("%d", &number2);
int lcm = findLCM(number1, number2);
printf("The LCM of %d and %d is: %d\n", number1, number2, lcm);
return 0;
  }
```

Output:
Enter the first number: 12
 Enter the second number: 18
 The LCM of 12 and 18 is: 36

9. Write a program to check if a given string is a palindrome using a function.

Answer:

```c
#include <stdio.h>
 #include <string.h>
int isPalindrome(char str[]) {
  int length = strlen(str);
  int start = 0;
  int end = length - 1;
```

```c
while (start < end) {
  if (str[start] != str[end]) {
  return 0; // Not a palindrome
  }
  start++;
  end--;
  }
return 1; // Palindrome
  }
int main() {
  char str[100];
printf("Enter a string: ");
  fgets(str, sizeof(str), stdin);
// Remove newline character from fgets
  str[strcspn(str, "\n")] = '\0';
if (isPalindrome(str)) {
  printf("%s is a palindrome.\n", str);
  } else {
  printf("%s is not a palindrome.\n", str);
  }
return 0;
  }
```

Output:
Enter a string: racecar
  racecar is a palindrome.
Enter a string: hello
  hello is not a palindrome.

10. Write a program to convert a decimal number to binary using a function.
Answer:
```c
#include <stdio.h>
void decimalToBinary(int decimal) {
  if (decimal == 0) {
  printf("Binary: 0");
  return;
  }
int binary[32];
  int index = 0;
while (decimal > 0) {
  binary[index] = decimal % 2;
  decimal = decimal / 2;
  index++;
  }
printf("Binary: ");
for (int i = index - 1; i >= 0; i--) {
  printf("%d", binary[i]);
```

```c
  }
  }
int main() {
  int decimal;
printf("Enter a decimal number: ");
  scanf("%d", &decimal);
decimalToBinary(decimal);
printf("\n");
return 0;
  }
```

  Output:
Enter a decimal number: 25
  Binary: 11001
Enter a decimal number: 0
  Binary: 0

Exercise-10

1. Write a program to find the length of a string without using the built-in string functions.

Answer:

```
#include <stdio.h>
int stringLength(const char* str) {
  int length = 0;
while (str[length] != '\0') {
  length++;
  }
return length;
  }
int main() {
  char str[100];
printf("Enter a string: ");
  scanf("%s", str);
int length = stringLength(str);
printf("Length of the string: %d\n", length);
return 0;
  }
```

Output:
Enter a string: Hello World
Length of the string: 11

2. Write a program to concatenate two strings without using the built-in string functions.

Answer:

```
#include <stdio.h>
void stringConcatenate(const char* str1, const char* str2, char* result) {
  int i = 0;
  int j = 0;
// Copy characters from the first string to the result
  while (str1[i] != '\0') {
  result[j] = str1[i];
  i++;
  j++;
  }
// Copy characters from the second string to the result
  i = 0;
  while (str2[i] != '\0') {
  result[j] = str2[i];
  i++;
  j++;
  }
// Add the null character to mark the end of the result string
  result[j] = '\0';
  }
int main() {
  char str1[100];
```

```c
  char str2[100];
  char result[200];
printf("Enter the first string: ");
  scanf("%s", str1);
printf("Enter the second string: ");
  scanf("%s", str2);
stringConcatenate(str1, str2, result);
printf("Concatenated string: %s\n", result);
return 0;
  }
```
Output:

Enter the first string:Hello

Enter the second string:World

Concatenated string: HelloWorld

3. Write a program to count the number of vowels in a given string.

Answer:

```c
#include <stdio.h>
int countVowels(const char* str) {
  int count = 0;
  int i = 0;
while (str[i] != '\0') {
  char currentChar = str[i];
// Check if the current character is a vowel
  if (currentChar == 'a' || currentChar == 'e' || currentChar == 'i' || currentChar == 'o' || currentChar == 'u'
  ||
  currentChar == 'A' || currentChar == 'E' || currentChar == 'I' || currentChar == 'O' || currentChar == 'U') {
  count++;
  }
i++;
  }
return count;
  }
int main() {
  char str[100];
printf("Enter a string: ");
  scanf("%s", str);
int vowelCount = countVowels(str);
printf("Number of vowels: %d\n", vowelCount);
return 0;
  }
```
Output:

Enter a string: Hello World

Number of vowels: 3

4. Write a program to reverse a given string.

Answer:

```c
#include <stdio.h>
```

```
void reverseString(char* str) {
  int length = 0;
// Calculate the length of the string
  while (str[length] != '\0') {
  length++;
  }
int start = 0;
  int end = length - 1;
// Reverse the string
  while (start < end) {
  // Swap characters at start and end positions
  char temp = str[start];
  str[start] = str[end];
  str[end] = temp;
// Move start towards the center and end towards the center
  start++;
  end--;
  }
  }
int main() {
  char str[100];
printf("Enter a string: ");
  scanf("%s", str);
reverseString(str);
printf("Reversed string: %s\n", str);
return 0;
  }
```

Output:

Enter a string:Hello World

Reversed string: dlroW olleH

5. Write a program to check if a given string is a palindrome.

Answer:

```
#include <stdio.h>
  #include <stdbool.h>
  #include <string.h>
bool isPalindrome(const char* str) {
  int length = strlen(str);
  int start = 0;
  int end = length - 1;
while (start < end) {
  if (str[start] != str[end]) {
  return false;
  }
start++;
  end--;
  }
```

```
return true;
  }
int main() {
   char str[100];
printf("Enter a string: ");
   scanf("%s", str);
if (isPalindrome(str)) {
   printf("The string is a palindrome.\n");
   } else {
   printf("The string is not a palindrome.\n");
   }
return 0;
   }
Output:
Enter a string: madam
The string is a palindrome.
```
6. Write a program to convert all lowercase characters in a string to uppercase.
Answer:
```
#include <stdio.h>
  #include <ctype.h>
void convertToLowercase(char* str) {
   int i = 0;
while (str[i] != '\0') {
   str[i] = toupper(str[i]);
   i++;
   }
   }
int main() {
   char str[100];
printf("Enter a string: ");
   scanf("%s", str);
convertToLowercase(str);
printf("Converted string: %s\n", str);
return 0;
   }
   Output:
Enter a string: Hello World
Converted string: HELLO WORLD
```
7. Write a program to count the occurrence of a specific character in a given string.
Answer:
```
#include <stdio.h>
int countOccurrence(const char* str, char target) {
   int count = 0;
   int i = 0;
while (str[i] != '\0') {
   if (str[i] == target) {
   count++;
```

```
    }
    i++;
    }
return count;
    }
int main() {
    char str[100];
    char target;
printf("Enter a string: ");
    scanf("%s", str);
printf("Enter the character to count: ");
    scanf(" %c", &target);
int occurrenceCount = countOccurrence(str, target);
printf("Number of occurrences of '%c': %d\n", target, occurrenceCount);
return 0;
    }
Output:
Enter a string: Hello World
Number of occurrences of 'o': 2
```

8. Write a program to find the frequency of each character in a string and display the result.
Answer:

```
#include <stdio.h>
#define MAX_SIZE 100
void findCharacterFrequency(const char* str) {
    int frequency[26] = {0}; // Assuming only lowercase alphabets (a-z)
int i = 0;
    while (str[i] != '\0') {
    if (str[i] >= 'a' && str[i] <= 'z') {
    int index = str[i] - 'a';
    frequency[index]++;
    }
    i++;
    }
printf("Character Frequencies:\n");
    for (int j = 0; j < 26; j++) {
    if (frequency[j] > 0) {
    printf("%c: %d\n", 'a' + j, frequency[j]);
    }
    }
    }
int main() {
    char str[MAX_SIZE];
printf("Enter a string: ");
    fgets(str, sizeof(str), stdin);
findCharacterFrequency(str);
return 0;
    }
```

Output:
Enter a string: Hello World
Character Frequencies:
　d: 1
　e: 1
　h: 1
　l: 3
　o: 2
　r: 1
　w: 1

9. Write a program to remove all the spaces from a given string.
Answer:

```c
#include <stdio.h>
void removeSpaces(char* str) {
  int i = 0;
  int j = 0;
while (str[i] != '\0') {
  if (str[i] != ' ') {
  str[j] = str[i];
  j++;
  }
  i++;
  }
  str[j] = '\0';
  }
int main() {
  char str[100];
printf("Enter a string: ");
  fgets(str, sizeof(str), stdin);
removeSpaces(str);
printf("String after removing spaces: %s\n", str);
return 0;
  }
```

Output:
Enter a string: man made
String after removing spaces: manmade

10. Write a program to check if two strings are anagrams of each other.
Answer:

```c
#include <stdio.h>
  #include <stdbool.h>
  #include <string.h>
#define MAX_SIZE 100
bool areAnagrams(const char* str1, const char* str2) {
  int count1[26] = {0}; // Assuming only lowercase alphabets (a-z)
  int count2[26] = {0};
```

```c
int length1 = strlen(str1);
    int length2 = strlen(str2);
if (length1 != length2) {
    return false;
    }
for (int i = 0; i < length1; i++) {
    if (str1[i] >= 'a' && str1[i] <= 'z') {
    count1[str1[i] - 'a']++;
    }
    if (str2[i] >= 'a' && str2[i] <= 'z') {
    count2[str2[i] - 'a']++;
    }
    }
for (int i = 0; i < 26; i++) {
    if (count1[i] != count2[i]) {
    return false;
    }
    }
return true;
    }
int main() {
    char str1[MAX_SIZE];
    char str2[MAX_SIZE];
printf("Enter the first string: ");
    fgets(str1, sizeof(str1), stdin);
printf("Enter the second string: ");
    fgets(str2, sizeof(str2), stdin);
if (areAnagrams(str1, str2)) {
    printf("The strings are anagrams.\n");
    } else {
    printf("The strings are not anagrams.\n");
    }
return 0;
    }
```
Output:
Enter the first string: listen
Enter the second string: silent
The strings are anagrams.

Exercise-11

1. Write a program to calculate the factorial of a given number using recursion.

Answer:

```c
#include <stdio.h>
unsigned long long factorial(unsigned int num) {
  if (num == 0)
  return 1;
  else
  return num * factorial(num - 1);
  }
int main() {
  unsigned int num;
printf("Enter a positive integer: ");
  scanf("%u", &num);
unsigned long long result = factorial(num);
printf("Factorial of %u is %llu\n", num, result);
return 0;
  }
```

Output:

Enter a positive integer: 5

  Factorial of 5 is 120

2. Write a program to find the nth Fibonacci number using recursion.

Answer:

```c
#include <stdio.h>
unsigned long long fibonacci(unsigned int n) {
  if (n <= 1)
  return n;
  else
  return fibonacci(n - 1) + fibonacci(n - 2);
  }
int main() {
  unsigned int n;
printf("Enter the value of n: ");
  scanf("%u", &n);
unsigned long long result = fibonacci(n);
printf("The %u-th Fibonacci number is: %llu\n", n, result);
return 0;
  }
```

Output:

Enter the value of n: 7

  The 7-th Fibonacci number is: 13

3. Write a program to calculate the sum of digits in a given number using recursion.

Answer:

```c
#include <stdio.h>
int sumOfDigits(int num) {
  if (num == 0)
  return 0;
```

```c
  else
  return (num % 10) + sumOfDigits(num / 10);
  }
int main() {
  int num;
printf("Enter a positive integer: ");
  scanf("%d", &num);
int result = sumOfDigits(num);
printf("Sum of digits in %d is %d\n", num, result);
return 0;
  }
```
Output:
Enter a positive integer: 12345
  Sum of digits in 12345 is 15

4. Write a program to reverse a string using recursion.
Answer:
```c
#include <stdio.h>
  #include <string.h>
void reverseString(char str[]) {
  int length = strlen(str);
if (length <= 1)
  return;
char temp = str[0];
  str[0] = str[length - 1];
  str[length - 1] = temp;
reverseString(str + 1);
  }
int main() {
  char str[100];
printf("Enter a string: ");
  fgets(str, sizeof(str), stdin);
// Remove newline character from fgets
  str[strcspn(str, "\n")] = '\0';
printf("Before reversing: %s\n", str);
reverseString(str);
printf("After reversing: %s\n", str);
return 0;
  }
```
Output:
Enter a string: Hello, World!
  Before reversing: Hello, World!
  After reversing: !dlroW ,olleH

5. Write a program to check if a given string is a palindrome using recursion.
Answer:
```c
#include <stdio.h>
  #include <stdbool.h>
  #include <string.h>
```

```c
bool isPalindrome(char *string, int start, int end) {
    // Base case: When the start index surpasses the end index
    if (start >= end) {
    return true;
    }

    // Recursive case: When the characters at start and end indices are equal
    if (string[start] == string[end]) {
    return isPalindrome(string, start + 1, end - 1);
    }

    return false;
    }
int main() {
    char string[100];
    printf("Enter a string: ");
    fgets(string, sizeof(string), stdin);

    // Remove the newline character from the input
    string[strcspn(string, "\n")] = '\0';
int length = strlen(string);
    bool result = isPalindrome(string, 0, length - 1);
if (result) {
    printf("The string '%s' is a palindrome.\n", string);
    } else {
    printf("The string '%s' is not a palindrome.\n", string);
    }
return 0;
    }
```
Output:
Enter a string: radar
    The string 'radar' is a palindrome.

6. Write a program to find the GCD (Greatest Common Divisor) of two numbers using recursion.
Answer:
```c
#include <stdio.h>
int gcd(int a, int b) {
    // Base case: When b is 0, the GCD is found
    if (b == 0) {
    return a;
    }

    // Recursive case: Calculate GCD using Euclidean algorithm
    return gcd(b, a % b);
    }
int main() {
    int num1, num2;
    printf("Enter two numbers: ");
```

```
  scanf("%d %d", &num1, &num2);

  int result = gcd(num1, num2);

  printf("The GCD of %d and %d is: %d\n", num1, num2, result);

  return 0;
  }
```
Output: Enter two numbers: 24 36
  The GCD of 24 and 36 is: 12

7. Write a program to calculate the power of a number using recursion.
Answer:
```
#include <stdio.h>
double power(double base, int exponent) {
  // Base case: exponent is 0
  if (exponent == 0) {
  return 1;
  }
// Recursive case: exponent is positive
  if (exponent > 0) {
  return base * power(base, exponent - 1);
  }
// Recursive case: exponent is negative
  if (exponent < 0) {
  return 1 / (base * power(base, -exponent - 1));
  }
  }
int main() {
  double base;
  int exponent;
  printf("Enter the base number: ");
  scanf("%lf", &base);
  printf("Enter the exponent: ");
  scanf("%d", &exponent);
double result = power(base, exponent);
  printf("%.2lf raised to the power of %d is: %.2lf\n", base, exponent, result);
return 0;
  }
```
Output:
Enter the base number: 2.5
  Enter the exponent: 3
  2.50 raised to the power of 3 is: 15.63
8. Write a program to print all possible permutations of a given string using recursion.
Answer:
```
#include <stdio.h>
  #include <string.h>
```

```c
void swap(char *x, char *y) {
  char temp = *x;
  *x = *y;
  *y = temp;
  }
void permutations(char *string, int left, int right) {
  if (left == right) {
  printf("%s\n", string);
  } else {
  for (int i = left; i <= right; i++) {
  swap((string + left), (string + i));
  permutations(string, left + 1, right);
  swap((string + left), (string + i)); // backtrack
  }
  }
  }
int main() {
  char string[100];
  printf("Enter a string: ");
  scanf("%s", string);

  int length = strlen(string);
  printf("All possible permutations of the string:\n");
  permutations(string, 0, length - 1);

  return 0;
  }
```
Output:

Enter a string: ABC
  All possible permutations of the string:
  ABC
  ACB
  BAC
  BCA
  CBA
  CAB

9. Write a program to find the sum of all elements in an array using recursion.

Answer:

```c
#include <stdio.h>
int arraySum(int arr[], int size) {
  // Base case: When the array size is 0, sum is 0
  if (size == 0) {
  return 0;
  }

  // Recursive case: Calculate sum of array elements
```

```
  return arr[size - 1] + arraySum(arr, size - 1);
  }
int main() {
  int arr[] = {1, 2, 3, 4, 5};
  int size = sizeof(arr) / sizeof(arr[0]);
int sum = arraySum(arr, size);
  printf("Sum of array elements: %d\n", sum);
return 0;
  }
```

Output:

Sum of array elements: 15

10. Write a program to solve the Tower of Hanoi problem using recursion.

Answer:

```
#include <stdio.h>
void towerOfHanoi(int n, char source, char auxiliary, char destination) {
  if (n == 1) {
  printf("Move disk 1 from %c to %c\n", source, destination);
  return;
  }
towerOfHanoi(n - 1, source, destination, auxiliary);
  printf("Move disk %d from %c to %c\n", n, source, destination);
  towerOfHanoi(n - 1, auxiliary, source, destination);
  }
int main() {
  int numDisks;
  printf("Enter the number of disks: ");
  scanf("%d", &numDisks);
printf("Tower of Hanoi solution:\n");
  towerOfHanoi(numDisks, 'A', 'B', 'C');
return 0;
  }
```

Output:

Enter the number of disks: 3
  Tower of Hanoi solution:
  Move disk 1 from A to C
  Move disk 2 from A to B
  Move disk 1 from C to B
  Move disk 3 from A to C
  Move disk 1 from B to A
  Move disk 2 from B to C
  Move disk 1 from A to C

Exercise-12

1. What is pointer and it's type?

Answer:

A pointer is a variable that stores the memory address of another variable. It allows direct access and manipulation of the value stored at that memory address. In C, pointers play a crucial role in various programming tasks, including dynamic memory allocation, passing parameters by reference, and working with arrays and strings.

In C, pointers have different types depending on the type of data they point to. Here are some commonly used pointer types:

1. **Pointer to int**: It stores the memory address of an integer variable. Declared using the syntax `int*`.

Example:

```
int* ptr; // Pointer to int
```

2. **Pointer to float**: It stores the memory address of a floating-point variable. Declared using the syntax `float*`.

Example:

```
float* ptr; // Pointer to float
```

3. **Pointer to char**: It stores the memory address of a character variable. Declared using the syntax `char*`.

Example:

```
char* ptr; // Pointer to char
```

4. **Pointer to array**: It stores the memory address of the first element of an array. Declared by specifying the array type followed by an asterisk.

Example:

```
int arr[5];
int* ptr = arr; // Pointer to the first element of the int array
```

5. **Pointer to structure**: It stores the memory address of a structure variable. Declared by specifying the structure type followed by an asterisk.

Example:

```
struct Person {
char name[20];
int age;
};
struct Person* ptr; // Pointer to struct Person
```

6. **Pointer to void**: It is a generic pointer that can store the memory address of any type. Useful in cases where the specific data type is unknown or can vary.

Example:

```
void* ptr; // Pointer to void
```

These are just a few examples of pointer types in C. Pointers are powerful tools that allow you to manipulate data efficiently by directly accessing memory locations. However, it's important to handle pointers carefully to avoid memory-related issues like segmentation faults and memory leaks.

2. What is Call by Value and Call by reference ?
Answer:
"Call by Value" and "Call by Reference" are two different mechanisms for passing arguments to functions in programming languages.

1. **Call by Value**: In Call by Value, a copy of the argument's value is passed to the function. Any changes made to the parameter inside the function do not affect the original argument in the calling function.
Example:

```c
void increment(int num) {
num++;
}
int main() {
  int x = 5;
  increment(x);
  printf("%d\n", x); // Output: 5 (unchanged)
  return 0;
}
```

In the above example, the `increment` function takes an argument `num` by value. Even though the `num` parameter is incremented inside the function, the original variable `x` in the `main` function remains unaffected.

2. **Call by Reference**: In Call by Reference, the memory address of the argument is passed to the function. Any changes made to the parameter inside the function affect the original argument in the calling function.
Example:

```c
void increment(int* num) {
(*num)++;
}
int main() {
  int x = 5;
  increment(&x);
  printf("%d\n", x); // Output: 6 (changed)
  return 0;
}
```

In the above example, the `increment` function takes an argument `num` as a pointer to an integer. By dereferencing the pointer using `*num`, we can modify the value stored at the memory address passed to the function. As a result, the original variable `x` in the `main` function is incremented.

In Call by Reference, changes made to the parameter inside the function directly impact the original argument. This mechanism is useful when you want to modify the original value of a variable or pass large data structures efficiently. Pointers are commonly used to implement Call by Reference.

Call by Value is simpler and involves making a copy of the value, ensuring that changes inside the function do not affect the original variable. It is used when you don't need to modify the original value or when dealing with small-sized variables.

The choice between Call by Value and Call by Reference depends on the requirements of the program and how you want the function to interact with the original data.

3. Write a program that concatenates two strings using pointers.
Answer:

```c
#include <stdio.h>
void concatenateStrings(char* str1, const char* str2) {
  // Move the pointer to the end of str1
  while (*str1 != '\0') {
   str1++;
   }
// Copy the characters from str2 to the end of str1
  while (*str2 != '\0') {
   *str1 = *str2;
   str1++;
   str2++;
   }
*str1 = '\0'; // Add the null character to mark the end of the concatenated string
  }
int main() {
  char str1[100];
  char str2[50];
printf("Enter the first string: ");
  scanf("%s", str1);
printf("Enter the second string: ");
  scanf("%s", str2);
concatenateStrings(str1, str2);
printf("Concatenated string: %s\n", str1);
return 0;
  }
```

Output:
Enter the first string:Hello
Enter the Second string:World
Concatenated string: HelloWorld

4. what is the use of pointer in C?
Answer:

Pointers in C have various uses and play a significant role in programming. Here are some important uses of pointers:

1. **Dynamic Memory Allocation:** Pointers allow dynamic memory allocation, enabling you to allocate memory dynamically during runtime using functions like `malloc`, `calloc`, and `real loc`. This flexibility is particularly useful when working with data structures of variable sizes or when memory needs to be allocated on-demand.

2. **Efficiently Working with Arrays:** Pointers facilitate efficient manipulation of arrays. They can be used to traverse, access, and modify array elements without the need for index-based operations. Additionally, pointers can be passed to functions, allowing modifications to be made directly to the original array.

3. **Passing Parameters by Reference:** Pointers enable passing parameters to functions by reference. This means that changes made to the parameters inside the function affect

the original variables in the calling code. It provides an alternative to passing by value and allows functions to modify variables directly.

4. Working with Strings: C does not have a built-in string data type, but rather represents strings as arrays of characters terminated by a null character (`'\0'`). Pointers are extensively used to manipulate and traverse strings, allowing operations like string concatenation, copying, and comparison.

5. Implementing Data Structures: Pointers are vital in implementing various data structures such as linked lists, trees, graphs, and dynamic data structures like stacks and queues. These data structures rely on pointers to establish relationships between nodes or elements and enable efficient memory management.

6. Accessing Hardware and I/O: Pointers provide a means to directly access and manipulate hardware registers, memory-mapped devices, and external resources. They are often used in low level programming or embedded systems development where precise control over hardware is required. Pointers are also useful for efficient input/output operations, such as reading and writing data to files.

7. Efficient Memory Management: Pointers allow you to efficiently manage memory by providing direct access to the memory location.

This enables operations like memory deallocation and reallocation when needed, optimizing memory usage and preventing memory leaks.

8. Implementing Algorithms and Data Manipulation: Pointers enable the implementation of complex algorithms and data manipulation operations. They facilitate operations like searching, sorting, and rearranging data structures efficiently by accessing and manipulating elements directly in memory.

By leveraging pointers, programmers gain control over memory, data structures, and resource management, allowing for efficient and flexible programming. However, working with pointers requires careful handling to avoid issues such as null pointer dereferences, memory leaks, or accessing invalid memory locations.

5. Write a program that dynamically allocates memory for an integer array of size n and then reads n integers from the user. Print the sum and average of these numbers using pointers.

Answer:

```c
#include <stdio.h>
#include <stdlib.h>
int main() {
 int n;
 int* numbers;
 int sum = 0;
 double average;
printf("Enter the number of integers: ");
 scanf("%d", &n);
numbers = (int*)malloc(n * sizeof(int));
if (numbers == NULL) {
 printf("Memory allocation failed!\n");
```

```
  return 1; // Exit the program indicating an error
  }
printf("Enter %d integers:\n", n);
  for (int i = 0; i < n; i++) {
  scanf("%d", &numbers[i]);
  sum += numbers[i];
  }
average = (double)sum / n;
printf("Sum: %d\n", sum);
  printf("Average: %.2lf\n", average);
free(numbers);
return 0;
  }
Output:
Sum: 150
  Average: 30.00
```

6. Write a program to calculate the factorial of a given number.

Answer:

```
#include <stdio.h>
unsigned long long factorial(int n) {
  unsigned long long result = 1;
if (n < 0) {
  return 0; // Factorial is undefined for negative numbers
  }
for (int i = 1; i <= n; i++) {
  result *= i;
  }
return result;
  }
int main() {
  int number;
printf("Enter a number: ");
  scanf("%d", &number);
unsigned long long fact = factorial(number);
printf("Factorial of %d = %llu\n", number, fact);
return 0;
  }
Output;
Enter a number: 5
Factorial of 5 = 120
```

7. Implement a program to check whether a given number is prime or not

Answer:

```
#include <stdio.h>
  #include <stdbool.h>
bool isPrime(int number) {
  if (number <= 1) {
```

```c
    return false; // Numbers less than or equal to 1 are not prime
  }
for (int i = 2; i * i <= number; i++) {
  if (number % i == 0) {
  return false; // Number is divisible by i, hence not prime
  }
  }
return true; // Number is prime
  }
int main() {
  int number;
printf("Enter a number: ");
  scanf("%d", &number);
if (isPrime(number)) {
  printf("%d is a prime number.\n", number);
  } else {
  printf("%d is not a prime number.\n", number);
  }
return 0;
  }
```
Output:
Enter a number: 17
17 is a prime number.

8. Write a program to find the sum of all elements in an array.
Answer:
```c
#include <stdio.h>
int main() {
  int arr[] = {10, 20, 30, 40, 50};
  int size = sizeof(arr) / sizeof(arr[0]);
  int sum = 0;
for (int i = 0; i < size; i++) {
  sum += arr[i];
  }
printf("Sum of array elements: %d\n", sum);
return 0;
  }
```

9. Implement a program to reverse a string without using any library functions.
Answer:
```c
#include <stdio.h>
void reverseString(char* str) {
  int length = 0;
// Find the length of the string
  while (str[length] != '\0') {
  length++;
  }
// Reverse the string
  for (int i = 0, j = length - 1; i < j; i++, j--) {
```

```c
  // Swap characters at positions i and j
  char temp = str[i];
  str[i] = str[j];
  str[j] = temp;
  }
  }
int main() {
  char str[100];
printf("Enter a string: ");
  scanf("%s", str);
reverseString(str);
printf("Reversed string: %s\n", str);
return 0;
  }
```
Output:
Enter a string: Language
Reversed string: egaugnaL

10. Write a program to find the largest and smallest elements in an array.

Answer:
```c
#include <stdio.h>
void findMinMax(int arr[], int size, int* min, int* max) {
  *min = arr[0]; // Assume the first element as the minimum
  *max = arr[0]; // Assume the first element as the maximum
for (int i = 1; i < size; i++) {
  if (arr[i] < *min) {
  *min = arr[i];
  }
  if (arr[i] > *max) {
  *max = arr[i];
  }
  }
  }
int main() {
  int arr[] = {10, 20, 5, 40, 30};
  int size = sizeof(arr) / sizeof(arr[0]);
  int min, max;
findMinMax(arr, size, &min, &max);
printf("Minimum element: %d\n", min);
  printf("Maximum element: %d\n", max);
return 0;
  }
```
Output:
Minimum element: 5
  Maximum element: 40

Exercise-13

1. what is the impotance of type casting in C

Answer:

- Data Conversion: Type casting allows you to convert a value from one data type to another. It is useful when you want to perform operations or assignments involving variables of different data types. For example, if you have an integer variable and you want to perform division with another variable of type float, you can use type casting to convert the integer to float before performing the division.
- Precision and Accuracy: Type casting allows you to control the precision and accuracy of arithmetic operations. For example, when dividing two integers in C, the result will be an integer, discarding any decimal part. However, if you want a floating-point result with decimal precision, you can use type casting to convert one of the operands to a floating-point type before performing the division.
- Compatibility: Type casting helps in ensuring compatibility between different data types. It allows you to explicitly specify the desired type of a value, which can be useful when passing arguments to functions or assigning values to variables of a different type. It helps prevent data loss or unintended behavior due to implicit type conversions.
- Expressions and Operations: Type casting allows you to control the behavior of expressions and operations involving different data types. By explicitly casting the operands, you can ensure that the operation is performed as expected and that the result is of the desired data type. It gives you more control over the behavior of your code.
- Pointer Conversions: Type casting is also important when working with pointers. It allows you to convert pointers between different data types, such as converting a pointer to void to a pointer of a specific type. This is useful when working with dynamically allocated memory or when dealing with generic pointer types.

2. Develop a C program that reads a floating-point number from the user and rounds it to the nearest integer using type casting. Display the rounded integer value.

Answer:

```
#include <stdio.h>
int main() {
  float floatingPoint;
  printf("Enter a floating-point number: ");
  scanf("%f", &floatingPoint);
int roundedInteger = (int)(floatingPoint + 0.5);
printf("Rounded integer value: %d\n", roundedInteger);
return 0;
 }
```

  Output:

Enter a floating-point number: 3.7
  Rounded integer value: 4

3. Write a C program that calculates the area of a circle. Prompt the user to enter the radius (a floating-point number) and display the area as a floating-point value using type casting.

Answer:

```
#include <stdio.h>
int main() {
  float radius;
```

```
printf("Enter the radius of the circle: ");
scanf("%f", &radius);
float area = 3.14159 * radius * radius;
printf("Area of the circle: %f\n", (float)area);
return 0;
}
```
Output:
Enter the radius of the circle: 2.5
  Area of the circle: 19.634949

Exercise-14

1. What is union in C?
Answer:

a union is a user-defined data type that allows multiple variables to share the same memory space. It enables storing different types of data in the same memory location. The memory allocated for a union is determined by the size of its largest member.

In a union, all members share the same memory location, and only one member can hold a value at a time. The size of a union is equal to the size of its largest member.

Unions are useful when you need to store different types of data in a single variable, but only one type of data will be used at a time. They provide a memory-efficient way to represent different data types without allocating separate memory for each member.

2. Define a union named "Shape" that can represent Square. The Square should have members for sides. Write a program to demonstrate the usage of this union.

Answer: The Square union has a member for the length of the sides. The program demonstrates the usage of this union:

```
#include <stdio.h>
union Shape {
  int sides;
};
int main() {
  union Shape square;
// Assigning values to the union member
  square.sides = 4;
printf("Square sides: %d\n", square.sides);
return 0;
}
```

In this program, we define a union named "Shape" that represents a Square. The union has a single member sides of type int.

In the main function, we create a variable square of type union Shape. We can assign and access values to/from the sides member of the union.

In this example, we assign a value of 4 to the sides member to represent a square with four equal sides. We then print the value of square.sides using printf.

The program demonstrates the usage of the union to represent a Square. The advantage of using a union is that it allows us to use the same memory space to store different types of data. However, it's important to note that modifying one member of the union may affect the value of other members since they share the same memory location.

3. Define a union named "Book" that can represent either a paperback book or a hardcover book. The paperback book should have members for title, author, and price, while the hardcover book should have members for title, author, and edition. Write a program to demonstrate the usage of this union and display the details of a book based on the user's choice.

Answer:

program that defines a union named "Book" to represent either a paperback book or a hardcover book. The Paperback book has members for title, author, and price, while the Hardcover book has members for title, author, and edition. The program demonstrates the usage of this union and allows the user to display the details of a book based on their choice:

```c
#include <stdio.h>
#define MAX_TITLE_LENGTH 100
#define MAX_AUTHOR_LENGTH 100
union Book {
  struct {
  char title[MAX_TITLE_LENGTH];
  char author[MAX_AUTHOR_LENGTH];
  float price;
  } paperback;
struct {
  char title[MAX_TITLE_LENGTH];
  char author[MAX_AUTHOR_LENGTH];
  int edition;
  } hardcover;
  };
int main() {
  union Book book;
  int choice;
printf("Enter book type:\n");
  printf("1. Paperback\n");
  printf("2. Hardcover\n");
  printf("Choice: ");
  scanf("%d", &choice);
switch (choice) {
  case 1:
  printf("Enter paperback book title: ");
  scanf(" %[^\n]s", book.paperback.title);
  printf("Enter author name: ");
  scanf(" %[^\n]s", book.paperback.author);
  printf("Enter price: ");
  scanf("%f", &book.paperback.price);
printf("\nBook Details:\n");
  printf("Title: %s\n", book.paperback.title);
  printf("Author: %s\n", book.paperback.author);
  printf("Price: %.2f\n", book.paperback.price);
  break;
case 2:
  printf("Enter hardcover book title: ");
```

```c
    scanf(" %[^\n]s", book.hardcover.title);
    printf("Enter author name: ");
    scanf(" %[^\n]s", book.hardcover.author);
    printf("Enter edition: ");
    scanf("%d", &book.hardcover.edition);
printf("\nBook Details:\n");
    printf("Title: %s\n", book.hardcover.title);
    printf("Author: %s\n", book.hardcover.author);
    printf("Edition: %d\n", book.hardcover.edition);
    break;
default:
    printf("Invalid choice.\n");
    }
return 0;
    }
```

In this program, we define a union named "Book" that represents either a Paperback book or a Hardcover book. The Paperback book is defined using a structure containing members for title, author, and price. The Hardcover book is defined using a structure containing members for title, author, and edition.

In the main function, we create a variable book of type union Book and a variable choice to store the user's choice.

The program prompts the user to enter the book type, either Paperback or Hardcover, by providing options 1 and 2. Based on the user's choice, it reads the corresponding details of the book using scanf and stores them in the appropriate members of the union.

Finally, it displays the details of the book based on the user's choice by accessing the members of the union and printing them using printf.

Here's an example usage:

Enter book type:
  1. Paperback
  2. Hardcover
  Choice: 1
  Enter paperback book title: The Catcher in the Rye
  Enter author name: J.D. Salinger
  Enter price: 10.99
Book Details:
  Title: The Catcher in the Rye
  Author: J.D. Salinger
  Price: 10.99

In this example, the user selects Paperback as the book type and enters the corresponding details. The program then displays the details of the Paperback book.

Exercise-15

1. Write a program that creates a text file and writes "Hello, World!" to it.

Answer:

```
#include <stdio.h>
int main() {
  FILE *file = fopen("output.txt", "w");
if (file == NULL) {
  printf("Failed to create the file.\n");
  return 1;
  }
fprintf(file, "Hello, World!");
fclose(file);
printf("File created and text written successfully.\n");
return 0;
  }
```

2. Write a program that reads a text file and displays its content on the console.

Answer:

```
#include <stdio.h>
int main() {
  FILE *file = fopen("input.txt", "r");
if (file == NULL) {
  printf("Failed to open the file.\n");
  return 1;
  }
char ch;
  while ((ch = fgetc(file)) != EOF) {
  printf("%c", ch);
  }
fclose(file);
return 0;
  }
```

3. Write a program that appends a new line of text to an existing text file.

Answer:

```
#include <stdio.h>
int main() {
  FILE *file = fopen("output.txt", "a");
if (file == NULL) {
  printf("Failed to open the file.\n");
  return 1;
  }
char text[100];
  printf("Enter the text to append: ");
  fgets(text, sizeof(text), stdin);
fprintf(file, "%s", text);
fclose(file);
printf("Text appended successfully.\n");
```

```c
return 0;
}
```

4. Write a program that counts the number of characters, words, and lines in a text file.

Answer:

```c
#include <stdio.h>
int main() {
  FILE *file = fopen("input.txt", "r");
if (file == NULL) {
  printf("Failed to open the file.\n");
  return 1;
}
int charCount = 0;
  int wordCount = 0;
  int lineCount = 0;
  char ch;
  int inWord = 0;
while ((ch = fgetc(file)) != EOF) {
  charCount++;
if (ch == ' ' || ch == '\t' || ch == '\n') {
  inWord = 0;
}
  else if (inWord == 0) {
  inWord = 1;
  wordCount++;
}
if (ch == '\n') {
  lineCount++;
}
}
fclose(file);
printf("Character count: %d\n", charCount);
  printf("Word count: %d\n", wordCount);
  printf("Line count: %d\n", lineCount);
return 0;
}
```

5. Write a program that copies the contents of one text file to another.

Answer:

```c
#include <stdio.h>
int main() {
  FILE *sourceFile = fopen("source.txt", "r");
  FILE *destinationFile = fopen("destination.txt", "w");
if (sourceFile == NULL || destinationFile == NULL) {
  printf("Failed to open the file.\n");
  return 1;
}
char ch;
  while ((ch = fgetc(sourceFile)) != EOF) {
```

```c
    fputc(ch, destinationFile);
    }
fclose(sourceFile);
    fclose(destinationFile);
printf("File copied successfully.\n");
return 0;
    }
```

6. Write a program that searches for a specific word in a text file and displays the line numbers where the word is found.

Answer:
```c
#include <stdio.h>
    #include <string.h>
#define MAX_LINE_LENGTH 100
int main() {
    FILE *file = fopen("input.txt", "r");
if (file == NULL) {
    printf("Failed to open the file.\n");
    return 1;
    }
char searchWord[50];
    printf("Enter the word to search: ");
    scanf("%s", searchWord);
char line[MAX_LINE_LENGTH];
    int lineNumber = 0;
    int found = 0;
while (fgets(line, MAX_LINE_LENGTH, file) != NULL) {
    lineNumber++;
    if (strstr(line, searchWord) != NULL) {
    printf("Word '%s' found at line %d\n", searchWord, lineNumber);
    found = 1;
    }
    }
if (!found) {
    printf("Word '%s' not found in the file.\n", searchWord);
    }
fclose(file);
return 0;
    }
```

7. Write a program that reads a binary file containing student records and displays the average marks of all students.

Answer:
```c
#include <stdio.h>
typedef struct {
    char name[50];
    int marks;
    } StudentRecord;
```

```c
int main() {
  FILE *file = fopen("student_records.bin", "rb");
if (file == NULL) {
  printf("Failed to open the file.\n");
  return 1;
  }
StudentRecord record;
  int totalMarks = 0;
  int numStudents = 0;
while (fread(&record, sizeof(StudentRecord), 1, file) == 1) {
  totalMarks += record.marks;
  numStudents++;
  }
fclose(file);
if (numStudents > 0) {
  float averageMarks = (float)totalMarks / numStudents;
  printf("Average marks of all students: %.2f\n", averageMarks);
  } else {
  printf("No student records found.\n");
  }
return 0;
  }
```

8. Write a program that encrypts the contents of a text file using a simple encryption algorithm.
Answer:
```c
#include <stdio.h>
#define MAX_LINE_LENGTH 100
void encrypt(char *line) {
  int i = 0;
  while (line[i] != '\0') {
  if (line[i] >= 'a' && line[i] <= 'z') {
  line[i] = 'z' - (line[i] - 'a');
  } else if (line[i] >= 'A' && line[i] <= 'Z') {
  line[i] = 'Z' - (line[i] - 'A');
  }
  i++;
  }
  }
int main() {
  FILE *inputFile = fopen("input.txt", "r");
  FILE *outputFile = fopen("output.txt", "w");
if (inputFile == NULL || outputFile == NULL) {
  printf("Failed to open the file.\n");
  return 1;
  }
char line[MAX_LINE_LENGTH];
while (fgets(line, MAX_LINE_LENGTH, inputFile) != NULL) {
  encrypt(line);
```

```c
int main() {
  FILE *file = fopen("student_records.bin", "rb");
if (file == NULL) {
  printf("Failed to open the file.\n");
  return 1;
  }
StudentRecord record;
  int totalMarks = 0;
  int numStudents = 0;
while (fread(&record, sizeof(StudentRecord), 1, file) == 1) {
  totalMarks += record.marks;
  numStudents++;
  }
fclose(file);
if (numStudents > 0) {
  float averageMarks = (float)totalMarks / numStudents;
  printf("Average marks of all students: %.2f\n", averageMarks);
  } else {
  printf("No student records found.\n");
  }
return 0;
  }
```

8. Write a program that encrypts the contents of a text file using a simple encryption algorithm.

Answer:

```c
#include <stdio.h>
#define MAX_LINE_LENGTH 100
void encrypt(char *line) {
  int i = 0;
  while (line[i] != '\0') {
  if (line[i] >= 'a' && line[i] <= 'z') {
  line[i] = 'z' - (line[i] - 'a');
  } else if (line[i] >= 'A' && line[i] <= 'Z') {
  line[i] = 'Z' - (line[i] - 'A');
  }
  i++;
  }
  }
int main() {
  FILE *inputFile = fopen("input.txt", "r");
  FILE *outputFile = fopen("output.txt", "w");
if (inputFile == NULL || outputFile == NULL) {
  printf("Failed to open the file.\n");
  return 1;
  }
char line[MAX_LINE_LENGTH];
while (fgets(line, MAX_LINE_LENGTH, inputFile) != NULL) {
  encrypt(line);
```

```c
    fputc(ch, destinationFile);
    }
fclose(sourceFile);
    fclose(destinationFile);
printf("File copied successfully.\n");
return 0;
    }
```

6. Write a program that searches for a specific word in a text file and displays the line numbers where the word is found.

Answer:
```c
#include <stdio.h>
    #include <string.h>
#define MAX_LINE_LENGTH 100
int main() {
    FILE *file = fopen("input.txt", "r");
if (file == NULL) {
    printf("Failed to open the file.\n");
    return 1;
    }
char searchWord[50];
    printf("Enter the word to search: ");
    scanf("%s", searchWord);
char line[MAX_LINE_LENGTH];
    int lineNumber = 0;
    int found = 0;
while (fgets(line, MAX_LINE_LENGTH, file) != NULL) {
    lineNumber++;
    if (strstr(line, searchWord) != NULL) {
    printf("Word '%s' found at line %d\n", searchWord, lineNumber);
    found = 1;
    }
    }
if (!found) {
    printf("Word '%s' not found in the file.\n", searchWord);
    }
fclose(file);
return 0;
    }
```

7. Write a program that reads a binary file containing student records and displays the average marks of all students.

Answer:
```c
#include <stdio.h>
typedef struct {
    char name[50];
    int marks;
    } StudentRecord;
```

```c
    fputs(line, outputFile);
    }
fclose(inputFile);
    fclose(outputFile);
printf("File encrypted successfully.\n");
return 0;
    }
```

9. Write a program that reads a CSV file containing student names and their respective marks and calculates the average marks for each student.

Answer:

```c
#include <stdio.h>
  #include <stdlib.h>
  #include <string.h>
#define MAX_LINE_LENGTH 100
  #define MAX_NAME_LENGTH 50
typedef struct {
  char name[MAX_NAME_LENGTH];
  int *marks;
  int numMarks;
  } Student;
void calculateAverage(Student *student) {
  int sum = 0;
  for (int i = 0; i < student->numMarks; i++) {
  sum += student->marks[i];
  }
  float average = (float)sum / student->numMarks;
  printf("Average marks for student %s: %.2f\n", student->name, average);
  }
int main() {
  FILE *file = fopen("student_data.csv", "r");
if (file == NULL) {
  printf("Failed to open the file.\n");
  return 1;
  }
char line[MAX_LINE_LENGTH];
  Student students[100];
  int numStudents = 0;
while (fgets(line, MAX_LINE_LENGTH, file) != NULL) {
  char *token = strtok(line, ",");
  strcpy(students[numStudents].name, token);
int numMarks = 0;
  students[numStudents].marks = malloc(100 * sizeof(int));
while (token != NULL) {
  token = strtok(NULL, ",");
  if (token != NULL) {
  students[numStudents].marks[numMarks] = atoi(token);
  numMarks++;
```

```
        }
    }

    students[numStudents].numMarks = numMarks;
    calculateAverage(&students[numStudents]);
numStudents++;
    }
fclose(file);
return 0;
    }
```

10. Write a program that deletes a specific line from a text file and creates a new file without the deleted line.

Answer:

```c
#include <stdio.h>
void deleteLine(const char* inputFile, const char* outputFile, int lineToDelete) {
  FILE* input = fopen(inputFile, "r");
  FILE* output = fopen(outputFile, "w");
if (input == NULL || output == NULL) {
  printf("Failed to open the file.\n");
  return;
  }
char line[1000];
  int lineNumber = 1;
while (fgets(line, sizeof(line), input)) {
  if (lineNumber != lineToDelete) {
  fputs(line, output);
  }
  lineNumber++;
  }
fclose(input);
  fclose(output);
printf("Line %d deleted successfully.\n", lineToDelete);
  }
int main() {
  const char* inputFile = "input.txt";
  const char* outputFile = "output.txt";
  int lineToDelete;
printf("Enter the line number to delete: ");
  scanf("%d", &lineToDelete);
deleteLine(inputFile, outputFile, lineToDelete);
return 0;
  }
```

Exercise-16

1. **Write a C program that dynamically allocates memory for an integer array of size 'x' entered by the user. Initialize the array with values from 1 to 'n' and display the array elements.**

Answer:

```c
#include <stdio.h>
#include <stdlib.h>
int main() {
  int x;
printf("Enter the size of the array: ");
  scanf("%d", &x);
int* arr = (int*)malloc(x * sizeof(int));
if (arr == NULL) {
  printf("Memory allocation failed!\n");
  return 1; // Exit the program indicating an error
  }
// Initialize array elements with values from 1 to 'x'
  for (int i = 0; i < x; i++) {
  arr[i] = i + 1;
  }
// Display array elements
  printf("Array elements: ");
  for (int i = 0; i < x; i++) {
  printf("%d ", arr[i]);
  }
  printf("\n");
free(arr);
return 0;
  }
```

Output:

Enter the size of the array: 5

Array elements: 1 2 3 4 5

2. **Implement a program that dynamically allocates memory for a string entered by the user. Reverse the string using dynamic memory allocation and display the reversed string.**

Answer:

```c
#include <stdio.h>
#include <stdlib.h>
#include <string.h>
char* reverseString(const char* str) {
  int length = strlen(str);
  char* reversedStr = (char*)malloc((length + 1) * sizeof(char));
if (reversedStr == NULL) {
  printf("Memory allocation failed!\n");
  return NULL;
  }
for (int i = 0; i < length; i++) {
  reversedStr[i] = str[length - i - 1];
  }
```

```c
reversedStr[length] = '\0'; // Add null character to mark the end of the reversed string
return reversedStr;
 }
int main() {
  char inputString[100];
printf("Enter a string: ");
  scanf("%s", inputString);
char* reversedString = reverseString(inputString);
if (reversedString != NULL) {
  printf("Reversed string: %s\n", reversedString);
  free(reversedString);
 }
return 0;
 }
```

Output:

Enter a string: Programming

Reversed string: gnimmargorP

3. Create a program that dynamically allocates memory for a 2D array of size m x n entered by the user. Initialize the array with random numbers and display the array elements.

Answer:

```c
#include <stdio.h>
 #include <stdlib.h>
 #include <time.h>
int main() {
  int m, n;
printf("Enter the number of rows (m): ");
  scanf("%d", &m);
printf("Enter the number of columns (n): ");
  scanf("%d", &n);
int** array = (int**)malloc(m * sizeof(int*));
if (array == NULL) {
  printf("Memory allocation failed!\n");
  return 1; // Exit the program indicating an error
 }
// Dynamically allocate memory for each row
 for (int i = 0; i < m; i++) {
  array[i] = (int*)malloc(n * sizeof(int));
  if (array[i] == NULL) {
  printf("Memory allocation failed!\n");
  return 1; // Exit the program indicating an error
 }
 }
// Initialize the array with random numbers
  srand(time(NULL)); // Seed the random number generator
  for (int i = 0; i < m; i++) {
  for (int j = 0; j < n; j++) {
  array[i][j] = rand();
```

```c
  }
 }
// Display the array elements
  printf("Array elements:\n");
  for (int i = 0; i < m; i++) {
  for (int j = 0; j < n; j++) {
  printf("%d\t", array[i][j]);
  }
  printf("\n");
  }
// Free dynamically allocated memory
  for (int i = 0; i < m; i++) {
  free(array[i]);
  }
  free(array);
return 0;
  }
```

Output:
Enter the number of rows: 3
Enter the number of columns:4
Array elements:
  18756 19537 13165 28505
  20553 13510 14804 6409
  29368 23879 32175 249

Exercise- 17

1. What is a preprocessor directive in C? Give an example.

Answer:

A preprocessor directive in C is a statement that gives instructions to the preprocessor, which is a separate step in the compilation process. Preprocessor directives begin with a # symbol and are evaluated before the compilation of the source code.

One common example of a preprocessor directive is #include. It is used to include the contents of another file, typically a header file, into the current source file. Here's an example:

#include <stdio.h>

In this example, the #include <stdio.h> directive tells the preprocessor to include the contents of the standard input/output (stdio) header file. This allows the program to use functions like printf and scanf for input and output operations.

Preprocessor directives are processed by the preprocessor before the actual compilation of the source code begins. They provide a way to modify the behavior of the compiler or include external files, making them a powerful tool for code organization, modularity, and customization in C programming.

2. How do you include a header file in your C program using a preprocessor directive? Provide an example.

Answer:

To include a header file in your C program using a preprocessor directive, you can use the #include directive followed by the name of the header file enclosed in angle brackets (<>) or double quotes (""). Here's an example:

#include <stdio.h>

In this example, the #include <stdio.h> directive is used to include the standard input/output (stdio) header file. This allows you to use functions like printf and scanf for input and output operations in your C program.

You can also include your own header files that you have created. For example, if you have a header file named "myheader.h" in the same directory as your C program, you can include it using:

#include "myheader.h"

The #include "myheader.h" directive tells the preprocessor to include the contents of the "myheader.h" file in your C program.

Including header files allows you to use functions, macros, and declarations defined in those files in your program, providing modularity, code reuse, and better organization of your code.

3. What is the purpose of the "#define" directive in C? Explain with an example.

Answer:

The #define directive in C is used to define symbolic constants or macros. It allows you to give a name to a constant value or to define a code snippet that can be used throughout your program. The #define directive is a preprocessor directive, and it is evaluated before the actual compilation of the code begins.

Here's an example to illustrate the purpose of the #define directive:

```
#include <stdio.h>
#define PI 3.14159
  #define MAX(a, b) ((a) > (b) ? (a) : (b))
int main() {
  printf("The value of PI is: %f\n", PI);
int num1 = 10, num2 = 20;
  int maxNum = MAX(num1, num2);
printf("The maximum of %d and %d is: %d\n", num1, num2, maxNum);
```

```
return 0;
}
```
In this example, the #define directive is used to define two constants and a macro:

#define PI 3.14159: This defines the symbolic constant PI with the value 3.14159. Whenever PI is used in the program, it will be replaced by its defined value, which is 3.14159. This provides a way to give a name to a constant value and make the code more readable.

#define MAX(a, b) ((a) > (b) ? (a) : (b)): This defines a macro named MAX that takes two arguments a and b. The macro compares the values of a and b and returns the maximum value. It allows you to write a concise and reusable code snippet for finding the maximum of two numbers.

In the main function, we use these #define directives. We print the value of PI using printf, and we find the maximum of two numbers (num1 and num2) using the MAX macro. The preprocessor replaces PI and MAX with their defined values during the preprocessing step.

The purpose of the #define directive is to enhance code readability, maintainability, and reusability by providing a way to define constants and macros in C programs. It allows you to avoid using magic numbers or repetitive code by giving names to constant values and creating code snippets that can be used multiple times.

4. How do you use the "#ifdef" and "#ifndef" directives in C? Provide a scenario where these directives can be useful.

Answer:

The #ifdef and #ifndef directives in C are used to conditionally compile parts of the code based on whether a particular macro is defined or not. These directives allow you to include or exclude specific sections of code during the compilation process.

Here's how #ifdef and #ifndef directives are used:

#ifdef: It checks if a specific macro is defined. If the macro is defined, the code block following #ifdef is included in the compilation process; otherwise, it is skipped.

```
#ifdef MACRO_NAME
  // Code to be compiled if MACRO_NAME is defined
  #endif
```

#ifndef: It checks if a specific macro is not defined. If the macro is not defined, the code block following #ifndef is included in the compilation process; otherwise, it is skipped.

```
#ifndef MACRO_NAME
  // Code to be compiled if MACRO_NAME is not defined
  #endif
```

The #ifdef and #ifndef directives in C are used to conditionally compile parts of the code based on whether a particular macro is defined or not. These directives allow you to include or exclude specific sections of code during the compilation process.

Here's how #ifdef and #ifndef directives are used:

#ifdef: It checks if a specific macro is defined. If the macro is defined, the code block following #ifdef is included in the compilation process; otherwise, it is skipped.

cCopy code

#ifdef MACRO_NAME // Code to be compiled if MACRO_NAME is defined #endif

#ifndef: It checks if a specific macro is not defined. If the macro is not defined, the code block following #ifndef is included in the compilation process; otherwise, it is skipped.

cCopy code

#ifndef MACRO_NAME // Code to be compiled if MACRO_NAME is not defined #endif

The #ifdef and #ifndef directives are commonly used for conditional compilation, allowing different parts of the code to be compiled based on specific conditions. They are often used in combination with the #define directive to control the compilation of specific features or to handle platform-specific code.
Here's an example scenario where #ifdef and #ifndef directives can be useful:

```
#include <stdio.h>
#define DEBUG_MODE
int main() {
  // ...
#ifdef DEBUG_MODE
  printf("Debug mode is enabled.\n");
  // Code specific to debug mode
  #endif
// ...
#ifndef RELEASE_VERSION
  printf("This is not a release version.\n");
  // Code specific to non-release version
  #endifc
// ...
return 0;
  }
```

In this example, the DEBUG_MODE macro is defined using #define, indicating that the code is being compiled in debug mode. The DEBUG_MODE section is compiled, and it prints a debug message.
The RELEASE_VERSION macro is not defined, so the code inside the #ifndef RELEASE_VERSION block is included in the compilation process. It prints a message indicating that it is not a release version.
By defining or undefining specific macros, you can control which parts of the code are included during compilation. This allows you to selectively enable or disable certain features, set different behavior based on compile-time conditions, or handle platform-specific code.

5. What is the purpose of the "#pragma" directive in C? Give an example of how it can be used.
Answer:

The #pragma directive in C is used to provide specific instructions or directives to the compiler. It is compiler-specific and can be used to control various aspects of the compilation process or to enable specific compiler features. The behavior and available directives of #pragma can vary between different compilers.
One common use of #pragma is to disable or suppress compiler warnings for specific code sections. This can be useful when you know that certain warnings are expected or not relevant for a particular piece of code.
Here's an example:

```
#include <stdio.h>
int main() {
  int num = -10;
#pragma GCC diagnostic push
  #pragma GCC diagnostic ignored "-Wsign-compare"
  if (num < 0) {
  printf("Negative number.\n");
  }
  #pragma GCC diagnostic pop
return 0;
  }
```

In this example, the #pragma directive is used with the GCC compiler to control the generation of warnings. The GCC diagnostic directives are used to push and pop the warning state, and the -Wsign-compare directive is used to ignore the specific warning related to signed/unsigned integer comparison.

With these #pragma directives, the compiler warning for the signed/unsigned integer comparison is temporarily suppressed within the marked code block. This allows the code to be compiled without generating the warning for that specific comparison.

6. How do you concatenate two strings using the preprocessor directives in C? Provide an example.

Answer:

In C, you cannot directly concatenate two strings using preprocessor directives alone. Preprocessor directives are evaluated before the actual compilation of the code begins, and they do not have the capability to perform string manipulation or concatenation.

However, you can use the preprocessor's stringification feature to concatenate two string literals at compile-time. The # operator, also known as the stringification operator, converts a macro parameter or a macro argument into a string literal.

Here's an example to illustrate how you can concatenate two string literals using the preprocessor:

```
#include <stdio.h>
#define CONCATENATE(a, b) a ## b
int main() {
  printf("%s\n", CONCATENATE("Hello", "World"));
return 0;
  }
```

In this example, the CONCATENATE macro is defined using the preprocessor directive #define. It takes two arguments, a and b. The ## operator is used to concatenate the two arguments into a single string literal.

In the main function, we call the CONCATENATE macro with the string literals "Hello" and "World". During the preprocessing step, the CONCATENATE macro is expanded, and the resulting string literal "HelloWorld" is passed as the argument to printf, which then prints it.

Interview Questions

1. What is C language?
2. Why is C language used?
3. What is the difference between C and C++?
4. What is the difference between C and Java?
5. What are the features of C language?
6. What are the data types in C language?
7. What are the control statements in C language?
8. What are the looping constructs in C language?
9. What is the purpose of header files in C language?
10. What is a pointer in C language?
11. What are the advantages of using pointers in C language?
12. What is the difference between call by value and call by reference?
13. How can you dynamically allocate memory in C language?
14. What are the different types of memory allocation in C language?
15. What is a structure in C language?
16. What is the use of typedef in C language?
17. How can you implement inheritance in C language?
18. What is the purpose of macros in C language?
19. How can you pass an array as an argument to a function in C language?
20. How can you print a string in C language?
21. How can you read a string in C language?
22. What are the different types of operators in C language?
23. What are the different types of I/O functions in C language?
24. What is a function in C language?
25. What is the difference between function declaration and function definition in C language?
26. How can you return multiple values from a function in C language?
27. What are the different types of storage classes in C language?
28. How can you print an integer without using the printf() function in C language?
29. What is the use of #include in C language?
30. What is the difference between compiler and interpreter in C language?
31. How can you handle run-time errors in C language?
32. What is the purpose of the exit() function in C language?
33. How can you convert a string to an integer in C language?
34. What is the use of getch() function in C language?
35. How can you copy one string to another in C language?
36. What is the purpose of the void keyword in C language?
37. What is the difference between pre-increment and post-increment in C language?
38. What is the purpose of the modulus operator (%) in C language?
39. How can you compare two strings in C language?
40. How can you find the length of a string in C language?
41. What is the difference between structure and union in C language?

42. What is the use of a bitwise operator in C language?
43. What is the use of a ternary operator in C language?
44. What are the different types of memory segments in C language?
45. What is the purpose of the break statement in C language?
46. What is the purpose of the continue statement in C language?
47. What is the purpose of the goto statement in C language?
48. How can you perform file handling in C language?
49. How can you read and write data from a file in C language?
50. What is the purpose of the fgetc() and fputc() functions in C language?
51. How can you create a user-defined header file in C language?
52. What is the purpose of the register keyword in C language?
53. How can you delete a file from the system in C language?
54. What is the purpose of the signal handling functions in C language?
55. What is the difference between text files and binary files in C language?
56. How can you generate random numbers in C language?
57. What is the purpose of the sizeof() operator in C language?
58. How can you sort an array in C language?
59. What is the purpose of the switch statement in C language?
60. What is the purpose of the while loop in C language?
61. What is the purpose of the do-while loop in C language?
62. How can you pass a function as an argument to another function in C language?
63. What is the purpose of the malloc() and free() functions in C language?
64. What is the purpose of the qsort() function in C language?
65. How can you implement exception handling in C language?
66. How can you create a child process in C language?
67. What is the purpose of the fseek() function in C language?
68. How can you check for the end of file in C language?
69. What is the purpose of the realloc() function in C language?
70. How can you check for the existence of a file in C language?
71. What is the purpose of the memcpy() function in C language?
72. What is the purpose of the strtok() function in C language?
73. How can you copy one file to another in C language?
74. What is the purpose of the strcpy() function in C language?
75. What is the purpose of the strcmp() function in C language?
76. How can you write a function in C language?
77. What are the different types of linking in C language?
78. How can you delete a directory in C language?
79. What is the purpose of the sprintf() function in C language?
80. How can you search for a string in C language?
81. What is the purpose of the strcat() function in C language?
82. What is the purpose of the assert() macro in C language?
83. How can you check for the existence of a directory in C language?
84. What is the purpose of the memmove() function in C language?

85. How can you create a thread in C language?

86. What is the purpose of the strchr() function in C language?

87. What is the purpose of the strstr() function in C language?

88. What is the purpose of the fread() and fwrite() functions in C language?

89. How can you generate a unique filename in C language?

90. How can you delete a file from a directory in C language?

91. What is the purpose of the setjmp() and longjmp() functions in C language?

92. What is the purpose of the alarm() function in C language?

93. What is the purpose of the ungetc() function in C language?

94. What is the purpose of the fopen() and fclose() functions in C language?

95. How can you create a dynamic linked library in C language?

96. What is the purpose of the fflush() function in C language?

97. How can you read and write data from a structure in C language?

98. How can you perform socket programming in C language?

99. How can you compare two structures in C language?

100. What is the purpose of the strtod() function in C language?